P9-DEG-662

THE POWERS THAT BE

PROCESSES OF RULING-CLASS DOMINATION IN AMERICA

G. WILLIAM DOMHOFF

VINTAGE BOOKS
A DIVISION OF RANDOM HOUSE   NEW YORK

Vintage Books Edition, January 1979

Library of Congress Cataloging in Publication Data
Domhoff, G. William.
   The powers that be.
   Includes index.
   1.   Elite (Social sciences)—United States.
2.   Power (Social sciences)   3.   United States—
Politics and government.   4.   United States—
Social policy.   I.   Title.
HN90.E4D65   1979b   301.44'92'0973   78–55633
ISBN 0–394–72649–9

Manufactured in the United States of America

ACKNOWLEDGMENTS

I am grateful to Jean Pohoryles for taking a chance on this book when it was only an outline, and to Susan Bolotin for many useful editorial suggestions and seeing it through to completion at Random House.

My deepest thanks to Harold Salzman, my research assistant during the time this book was being written, for his invaluable help on both substantive and editorial tasks, including the final typing of the manuscript on the computer. The assistance of Mr. Salzman was made possible by grants from the Research Committee of the Academic Senate of the University of California, Santa Cruz, and I am grateful to that committee for its support of my research efforts.

Finally, my appreciation to Maurice Zeitlin, Derek Shearer, Thomas R. Dye, Kim McQuaid and Calvin S. Hall for their helpful suggestions on the first draft of the manuscript.

TO CALVIN, TEACHER AND FRIEND

CONTENTS

This book presents a new theory of how the owners and managers of large banks and corporations dominate the United States. As such, it is an evolution, not a repetition, of the concepts and findings in my earlier books. *Who Rules America?* (1967) described the sociological structure of the ruling class, using the overrepresentation of its members in economic and governmental posts, as well as its disproportionate wealth and income, as the major evidence of ruling-class power. The book paid only secondary attention to the process of domination. *The Higher Circles* (1970) contained an analysis of how important public policies are created and implemented, but that is only one aspect of the multifaceted problem of domination. *Fat Cats and Democrats* (1972) showed how big businesspeople dominate the party system, which is again only one aspect of a larger picture. *The Bohemian Grove and Other Retreats* (1974) demonstrated the cohesiveness and class consciousness of the capitalist class, whose relationships with government and subordinate classes will be the subject of this book. Finally, *Who Really Rules* (1978) presented an analysis of how corporate leaders dominate decisions of concern to them in local politics, but it does not directly confront the larger issues which are the subject of this present book. While bits and pieces of these previous book-length efforts are incorporated in the perspective to be elaborated in this book, heretofore this analysis has appeared only in a briefer and more unfinished form in sociological journals.[1]

The book begins with a general overview of the ruling class and the study of power in America. This provides a framework for considering the specific processes through which the ruling class dominates the government and underlying population within the territory or "state" known as the United States. Chapters 2 through 5 present a detailed theoretical and empirical analysis of the four different processes that I believe can be isolated and identified as the critical ones in explaining the exact nature of rule by the corporate rich. I am hopeful that these chapters provide a thorough answer to the many academic and journalistic commentators who claim that proponents of the ruling-class view are not able to articulate the means by which the ruling class is alleged to rule.

The Powers That Be is written as an interpretative theoretical essay rather than as a systematic survey of all aspects of politics and government. It is meant to be representative, rather than comprehensive, in the evidence it cites and in its selection of spokespersons for other theoretical positions. The subtitle— Processes of Ruling-Class Domination in America—should be taken as an accurate statement of the book's contents. Although I will briefly mention in the first chapter the several theoretical questions encountered in the study of the American ruling class,

1. "Some Friendly Answers to Radical Critics," *The Insurgent Sociologist*, Winter, 1972; "State and Ruling Class in Corporate America," *The Insurgent Sociologist*, Spring, 1974.

I will be focusing on only one of them, the ways in which the ruling class dominates this nation. In stressing this qualification, I am not implying that there are no common denominators in corporate capitalist domination of various nation-states around the world. I am only saying that the common denominators are not my primary focus.

In presenting a new viewpoint, this book of necessity criticizes other perspectives while encompassing some of their insights. Previously the focus of my criticisms has been almost exclusively on the pluralist theory of power in America, which is the prevailing paradigm within political science and political sociology.[2] To a lesser extent, I have critiqued the elitist theory of power, as exemplified by C. Wright Mills' *The Power Elite*. Here, however, I also will point out some of the shortcomings in recent Marxian works on the relationship between state and ruling class. The generalizations made by some Marxists about power in the United States on the basis of European experience or Marxist-Leninist texts are often as far from the mark as the conclusions pluralists draw from narrow case studies which ignore the class structure and organizational context that encompasses decision-making.[3]

Although the book will be critical of recent Marxist views of America at several points, it does share their premise that social classes are central to an analysis of power in America. I believe most political and economic problems in the United States must

2. For my specific criticism of leading pluralist works, see both "Where a Pluralist Goes Wrong," *The Higher Circles* (Random House, 1970), and *Who Really Rules: New Haven and Community Power Re-Examined* (Trans-Action Books and Goodyear Publishing Co., 1978).

3. Specifically, I will be criticizing the line of thinking which derives from Nicos Poulantzas, *Political Power and Social Classes* (New Left Books, 1973); Claus Offe, "Structural Problems of the Capitalist State," in Klaus von Beyme, ed., *German Political Studies* (Sage Publications, 1974); and David Gold et al., "Recent Developments in Marxist Theories of the Capitalist State," *Monthly Review*, November, 1975.

be understood in terms of the conflicts and compromises between the interests of two basic social classes that are rooted in the social organization of production. Those two classes are the ruling class, which owns and manages the major business enterprises, and the working class, which owns no income-producing property.[4] In a fundamental sense, then, my views belong within a "class-hegemony paradigm." They are in contrast to the pluralist and elitist frameworks, for the pluralist view emphasizes shifting coalitions of interest groups focused on specific issues as the key to understanding power, while the elitist perspective turns attention toward the organizational interests of large-scale bureaucratic institutions.[5]

Although the class-hegemony framework stresses the need to understand classes in relationship to one another, my emphasis is nonetheless on the ruling capitalist class, for it is the major initiator of action. It usually sets the terms of the interaction with the working class. This point is important to stress because many Marxian analysts, in their eagerness to see the working class replace capitalism with socialism, have failed to understand the primacy of the ruling class in analyzing the functioning of the present system. This point has been made very forcefully by one of the leading New Left thinkers of the 1960's, David Horowitz:

That Marx's sociological model has been subject to widespread misunderstanding can be seen at a glance in the fact that the Marxian

4. But not all problems can be understood solely in class terms. For an excellent study of how class interacts with religious, ethnic and regional considerations in the United States, see Richard Hamilton, *Class and Politics in the United States* (Wiley & Sons, 1972).

5. For an articulation of the assumptions, emphases and weaknesses of the pluralist, elitist and class-hegemony paradigms, see Robert R. Alford, "Paradigms of Relations Between State and Society," in Leon N. Lindberg et al., eds., *Stress and Contradiction in Modern Capitalism* (D.C. Heath and Co., 1975).

concept of class is almost exclusively discussed in terms of the proletariat and its revolutionary potential, whereas the operative group in terms of the *functioning* and *development* of the capitalist system (the subject of Marx's major work) is not the proletariat at all, but the *capitalist ruling class.*[6]

Following the lead suggested by Horowitz, this book will focus on the ruling class, rather than the working class, in attempting to explain how the United States is ruled. This does not deny that there is "class struggle." Nor does it leave consideration of the working class out of the picture. The effects of the working class will be seen in the policies and propaganda efforts through which the ruling class reacts to working-class challenges.

   The Powers That Be is dedicated to the teacher, friend and colleague who encouraged and helped me the most as a young academician, Calvin S. Hall. To him I owe a great deal.

—G. William Domhoff
Santa Cruz, California
February 1, 1978

6. David Horowitz, "A Note on Marx's Theory of Class," in his *The Fate of Midas and Other Essays* (Ramparts Press, 1973), p. 105. The italics are in the original.

THE POWERS THAT BE

The Ruling Class and the Problem of Power

On top of the gradually merging social layers of blue- and white-collar workers who comprise the working class and make up 85–90 percent of the population, there sits a very small social upper class which comprises at most 0.5 percent of the population and has a very different lifestyle and source of income from the rest of us. Many Americans are not even aware of the existence of this upper class. They are used to thinking of the highly paid and highly visible doctors, architects, television actors, corporate managers, writers, government officials and experts who stand between the working class and the upper class as the highest level of the social pecking order. The "rich people," if they come to mind at all, are thought of as a few wealthy eccentrics, such as Howard Hughes, who happened to strike it rich; or as the occasional wealthy families, such as the Rockefellers or Mellons or Du Ponts, which are thought to be a remnant of another age; or as the handful of playboys or jet setters who are bent on squandering the little that remains from once-significant family fortunes.

But "the rich" in the United States are not a handful of discontented eccentrics, jet setters and jaded scions who have been pushed aside by the rise of corporations and governmental bureaucracies. They are instead full-fledged members of a thriving social class which is as alive and well as it has ever been. Members of this privileged class, according to sociological and journalistic studies, live in secluded neighborhoods and well-guarded apartment complexes, send their children to private boarding schools, announce their teen-age daughters to the world by means of debutante teas and gala ballroom dances, play backgammon and dominoes at their exclusive social clubs and travel all over the world on their numerous junkets and vacations. They are active as executives and directors in major banks and corporations, as partners in large law firms, as directors of foundations, universities and cultural centers, and in numerous high-status professions. Some even involve themselves in the political fray, where they are referred to variously as "patricians," "Brahmins," "aristocrats" and "bourbons," depending upon the "age" of their money and the part of the country from which they come.[1]

There is also in America, as different types of studies show, an extremely distorted distribution of wealth that has remained relatively constant throughout the nineteenth and twentieth centuries. For selected years between 1953 and 1969, the top one percent of the population has owned between 25 percent and 30 percent of all privately held material wealth, including from 50–86 per-

1. For various portraits of the upper class, see Dixon Wecter, *The Saga of American Society* (Charles Scribner's Sons, 1937); E. Digby Baltzell, *Philadelphia Gentlemen: The Making of a National Upper Class* (Free Press, 1958); and Stephen Birmingham, *The Right People* (Little, Brown and Co., 1968).

cent of all corporate stock.[2] That is not quite the whole story, however, for a closer look at the top one percent shows that a mere 0.5 percent have most of the wealth in that category: "The richest 0.5 percent of the United States population has consistently held about 22.0 percent of personal wealth over the last thirty years."[3] The foregoing estimates were developed from studies of the estates of deceased wealthholders; a study for 1962, using survey information developed by the government from interviews with a sample of consumers, estimated that the top 0.5 percent of families held an even higher percent of the wealth, 25.8 percent.[4] Adults with a net worth of $1 million or more in 1969, who are at the core of the wealthy class, make up 0.1 percent of the adult population and have 9.6 percent of the total net worth.[5] All of these figures, it should be stressed, are considered conservative estimates, for good information on this touchy topic is hard to obtain.

As for income, the maldistribution is not quite as bad. In recent years the top 5 percent of income earners, most of whom are wealthy to begin with, have received 14–16 percent of all money income in the United States.[6] Although there are consider-

2. Jonathan H. Turner and Charles E. Staines, *Inequality: Privilege and Poverty in America* (Goodyear Publishing Co., 1976), p. 39, Table 13. This book presents the most recent and careful analysis of the several studies that have been done on wealth. The figures presented in this paragraph as percentage of wealth are in terms of net worth estimates (assets less debt). The most important recent study of top wealthholders reported by Turner and Staines is by James D. Smith and Stephen D. Franklin, "The Concentration of Personal Wealth, 1922–1969," *American Economic Review*, May, 1974.

3. *Ibid.*, p. 38.

4. *Ibid.*, p. 22, Table 5.

5. *Ibid.*, p. 43, Table 16.

6. *Ibid.*, p. 51, Table 2.

able data on income distribution, only one study attempts to estimate the percentage of yearly income that goes to the very wealthy. In that study, for the year 1958, it was estimated that the top 1.5 percent of wealthholders, those with assets of $60,000 or more, received 13 percent of the total income for that year. The percentage rose to 24 if income from capital gains is included. The estimate is considered a conservative one for several reasons, including the allocation of all Social Security income to the lower 98.5 percent of wealthholders.[7]

It is not hard for most of us to imagine that the small social upper class uncovered in sociological research is made up of the top wealthholders revealed in wealth and income studies. However, it is not necessary to rely on our imaginations, for it is possible to do empirical studies linking the one category to the other, thereby demonstrating that the "economic class" of large capitalists is one and the same with the highest "status group" or "social class" in the United States, as would be expected by class-hegemony theorists. The first systematic studies along this line were reported by sociologist E. Digby Baltzell, who showed that the wealthiest people of Philadelphia are also the people who send their children to expensive private schools, belong to exclusive social clubs and list in the "blue book" of the upper class, the *Social Register*, which is also one of the best indicators of upper-class standing.[8] Looking beyond Philadelphia to the nation as a whole, Baltzell found that nine of the ten very richest men at the turn of the century were listed in the *Social Register*. He also found that over 75 percent of the wealthy families in Ferdinand Lundberg's 1937 classic, *America's Sixty Families*, had easily traceable descendants (the same given and surnames as the family founder) in the *Social Register*, and that 87 of the families chron-

7. James D. Smith, "An Estimate of the Income of the Very Rich," *Papers in Quantitative Economics* (Univ. of Kansas Press, 1968).

8. Baltzell, *op. cit.*

icled in Gustavus Myers' *History of the Great American Fortunes* had descendants listed in that register.[9] Another sociologist, C. Wright Mills, compiled a list of the 90 richest men for the year 1900. He found that roughly half of those on the list had descendants in the New York, Boston or Philadelphia *Social Register* for 1940.[10]

In most countries, it would be taken for granted that a social upper class with a highly disproportionate amount of wealth and income is a ruling class with domination over the government. How else, it would be argued, could such a tiny network of families possess so much if it didn't have its hooks into government? After all, isn't "power" and "rulership" inferred from various value distributions, such as those for wealth and income, which are merely the outcomes of struggles and conflicts over how the social product is to be produced and how it is to be divided? Isn't politics about "who gets what," with the "when, where and how" as subsidiary questions when it comes to the shape of the power structure?

Not so in the United States today. In a nation that always has denied the existence of social classes and class conflict, and overestimated the degree of social mobility, systematic information on the persistent inequality of wealth and income tends to get lost from public and academic debate.[11] Besides, most social scientists, being of a pluralist persuasion, believe that many different groups, including organized labor, farmers, consumers and middle-class environmentalists, have a hand in political decisions

9. *Ibid.*, pp. 36–40.

10. C. Wright Mills, *The Power Elite* (Oxford Univ. Press), 1956, p. 117.

11. For historical information on the stability of the wealth distribution and the modest degree of social mobility, see Jackson Turner Main, *The Social Structure of Revolutionary America* (Princeton Univ. Press, 1965); Edward Pessen, ed., *Three Centuries of Social Mobility in America* (D.C. Heath and Co., 1974); and William Miller, *Men and Business* (Harvard Univ. Press, 1952).

—if not since the first years of the republic, at least since the Progressive Era and the New Deal. There is no such thing as a ruling class in America, or so we are assured by leading academicans, journalists and other public figures.

We can begin to understand this reaction to wealth and income statistics if we realize that the predominant emphasis in American ideology is on the "process" by which things are done—democracy in government, equality of opportunity in education, fairness before the law—and not on "outcomes." The emphasis on outcomes, implying as it does a possible bias toward social egalitarianism, was anathema to most of the founding fathers, and it is anathema to the corporate business community of today. A special commentary in *Business Week* in December 1975 went so far as to charge that the new egalitarian movement of the 1970's was actually authoritarian in nature and would wreck the economic system if it were able to substitute equality of outcomes for equality of opportunity.[12]

The emphasis on process in American thinking appears in the social sciences as a theory of power which insists that power can be known only by seeing it in action. That is, we must study the process of power, rather than infer power from outcomes. Who benefits, the very essence of a power struggle, is hardly considered. This viewpoint is epitomized in the writings of Robert A. Dahl, one of the two or three most eminent political theorists of the past two decades. In a sharp critique of sociologists Floyd Hunter and C. Wright Mills, both of whom believed on the basis of their studies that a small "power structure" or "power elite" dominated in the United States, Dahl rejected their evidence and argument because "I do not see how anyone can suppose that he has established the dominance of a specific group in a community or a nation without basing his analysis on the careful

12. "Egalitarianism: Threat to a Free Market," *Business Week*, December 1, 1975, p. 62.

examination of a series of concrete decisions." He went on to say that he found it a "remarkable and indeed astounding fact that neither Professor Mills nor Professor Hunter has seriously attempted to examine an array of specific cases to test his major hypothesis."[13] Not everyone, of course, has held to such an extreme emphasis on process within American social science, but enough have that it was somewhat heretical when a mainstream political scientist, William C. Mitchell, wrote in 1969: "Let us try defining power not as one who makes decisions but as who gets how much from the system. Those who acquire the most goods, services, and opportunities are those who have the most power."[14]

There are philosophical and methodological difficulties with a conceptualization of power and power indicators that focuses exclusively on process. However, rather than enter into an argument over these abstract points, I am going to set aside these differences of philosophy and method for purposes of this book.[15] I will accept the challenge presented by the dominant social-science paradigm and concentrate on the process by which the ruling class in the United States dominates government and subordinates other social classes. Putting aside the argument that we can infer power from the distributions of wealth, income, health, education and other benefits sought by members of American society, I will suggest that there are four general processes through which economically and politically active members of

13. Robert A. Dahl, "A Critique of the Ruling Elite Model," *American Political Science Review*, June, 1958, p. 466.

14. William C. Mitchell, "The Shape of Political Theory to Come: From Political Sociology to Political Economy," in Seymour M. Lipset, ed., *Politics and the Social Sciences* (Oxford Univ. Press, 1969), p. 114.

15. For general discussion of the problems of conceptualizing power, see Steven Lukes, *Power* (The Macmillan Co., 1974); Robert R. Alford and Roger Friedland, "Political Participation and Public Policy," *Annual Review of Sociology*, 1, (1975); and G. William Domhoff, *Who Really Rules*, *op. cit.*, chapter 4.

the ruling class, working with the aid of highly trained and carefully selected employees, are able to dominate the United States at all levels. I call these four processes:

1. *The special-interest process,* which comprises the various means utilized by wealthy individuals, specific corporations and specific sectors of the economy in influencing government to satisfy their narrow, short-run needs;
2. *The policy-formation process,* which is the means by which general policies of interest to the ruling class as a whole are developed and implemented;
3. *The candidate-selection process,* which has to do with the ways members of the ruling class ensure that they have "access" to the politicians who are elected to office;
4. *The ideology process,* which involves the formation, dissemination and enforcement of the assumptions, beliefs and attitudes that permit the continued existence of policies and politicians favorable to the wealth, income, status and privileges of members of the ruling class.

These four processes are separate from one another, but they do not run simply and smoothly along four isolated and easily observable sociological paths. Although there is some specialization of function among people and institutions, there also is overlap in the sociological networks which sustain each of the processes, as will become clear as the analysis unfolds. Nor do the four processes operate without conflict. Conflict is endemic to much of American political life, even though it must be remembered that there is often more smoke than fire in many of the controversies which engage the attention of newspaper readers and television audiences.[16] Indeed, one of the advantages of

16. Douglass Cater, *Power in Washington* (Random House, 1964), p. 241.

the four-process viewpoint to be presented here is that it makes it possible to sort out different kinds of conflicts and assess the degree to which they actually contradict a ruling-class theory of the American power structure. Many conflicts merely involve the division of profits within the ruling class. Some involve sacrificing the short-run interests of specific corporations or industries to the general and long-run interests of big businesspeople as a whole. Others involve no more than personal ambition and personality conflicts among those seeking further fame or fortune. Some involve policy differences between different segments of the ruling class. There are even a few occasions when the ever-present differences between the working class and the ruling class emerge into political conflicts which raise potential challenges to class rule. Within the schema to be presented here, account can be taken of the considerable amount of day-to-day political conflict which many social scientists see as prima facie evidence against a ruling-class perspective.

Before describing each of these four processes and their functioning, it is necessary to define the terms "state," "ruling class" and "power elite." It will then be possible to answer in a brief way several commonly raised objections to ruling-class theory that are preliminary to any discussion of the processes through which an alleged ruling class dominates the state.

"State" is a concept with three levels of meaning. At the most visible level, the state is a "sovereign political territory."[17] It is a nation-state, such as the United States or France. However, the state as a sovereign political territory is maintained by a "governmental system" or "state apparatus." This is the second meaning of "state," and it includes all aspects of the formal system of government—executive, legislative, judiciary, military and

17. Harold Lasswell and Abraham Kaplan, *Power and Society* (Yale Univ. Press, 1950), p. 181.

police.[18] Most important, however, the "state" is a state of mind, and its essence involves a common will on the part of the people within a given territory to unite for the common defense of that territory.[19] The "state," then, is ultimately defined by a common allegiance (patriotism), which is expressed in a willingness to accept the governmental system and to defend the common territory. The "state" as governmental apparatus and as a state of mind are thus embodied in the definition of the state as "a sovereign political territory."

By a ruling class I mean a clearly demarcated social class which has "power" over the government (state apparatus) and underlying population within a given nation (state). Evidence for the "power" of a ruling class can be found in such indicators as:

1. A disproportionate amount of wealth and income as compared to other social classes and groups within the state;
2. A higher standing than other social classes within the state on a variety of well-being statistics ranging from infant mortality rates to educational attainments;
3. Control over the major social and economic institutions of the state;
4. Domination over the governmental processes of the country.

This conception of a ruling class does not differ greatly from the views of other social scientists. For example, Marxian definitions of a ruling class speak in terms of a social class that controls the major means of production in a given society, whatever the legal forms of that control may be. A social class that can pass

18. Ralph Miliband, *The State in Capitalist Society* (Basic Books, 1969), p. 54.
19. Schlomo Avineri, *Hegel's Theory of the Modern State* (Cambridge Univ. Press, 1972), pp. 40–45.

on privileges to its children, direct investments to areas of its choosing, and divide the social product among the classes of society, giving itself a disproportionately large share, is a "ruling class" in a Marxian view.[20] Non-Marxian definitions differ only in that they do not stress ownership or control of the means of production as an integral factor in ruling-class domination. For example, Daniel Bell speaks of a ruling class as a power-wielding group with a continuity of interests and a community of interests.[21] E. Digby Baltzell writes in terms of an upper class that contributes members "to the most important, goal-integrating elite positions." For Baltzell, a ruling class is an upper class which can perpetuate its power "in the world of affairs, whether in the bank, the factory, or in the halls of the legislature."[22]

Generally speaking, then, there is considerable agreement that a ruling class is a social class that subordinates other social classes to its own profit or advantage. However, none of the definitions prescribe how this subordination takes place, nor who is directly involved in the process. To understand the how and who, it is necessary to introduce the concept of a "power elite." I define the power elite as the leadership group or operating arm of the ruling class. It is made up of active, working members of the ruling class and high-level employees in institutions controlled by members of the ruling class. It is members of this power elite or leadership group who dominate within each of the four processes that will be analyzed in the following chapters.

C. Wright Mills first introduced the concept of a power elite

20. For a consideration of what Marx and Engels wrote on the subject, see Ross Gandy, "More on the Nature of Soviet Society," *Monthly Review*, March, 1976, from which several of the phrases in this paragraph are taken. A summary of the Marxist view can be found in Charles H. Anderson, *The Political Economy of Social Class* (Prentice-Hall, 1974).

21. Daniel Bell, *The End of Ideology* (Free Press, 1969), chapters 2 and 3.

22. Baltzell, *op. cit.*, p. 405.

into the sociological literature as a substitute for "ruling class." Mills made this substitution because he thought the ruling class of big property owners and corporate executives had been transformed since the Great Depression and World War II by the addition of "political outsiders" (executive-branch appointees) and "warlords" (military leaders) into the highest circles of leadership and decision.[23] However, in the way I have redefined the term and used it over the past ten years (as the leadership arm of the ruling class), it is more akin to what Baltzell means by "the establishment," for it emphasizes that "while an establishment will always be dominated by upper-class members, it also must be constantly rejuvenated by new members of the elite who are in the process of acquiring upper-class status."[24]

The difference between Mills' definition and mine lies in the fact that 1) I do not assume *a priori* that any institutionally based group is by definition part of the power elite, as Mills did in so designating leaders within corporate, military and governmental bureaucracies; and 2) I have grounded the power elite in a social class. Using this approach, it is possible to determine empirically which parts of the economy and government can be considered direct outposts of the ruling class by virtue of disproportionate participation by members of the power elite. Proceeding in this fashion I was able to show in earlier research that the power elite as I define it has a membership very similar to that hypothesized by Mills.[25]

Both of these concepts—ruling class and power elite—are important in an examination of how America is ruled, for they

23. Mills, *op. cit.*

24. E. Digby Baltzell, *The Protestant Establishment* (Random House, 1964), p. 8.

25. For a summary of this evidence, see my "The Power Elite and Its Critics," in G. William Domhoff and Hoyt B. Ballard, eds., *C. Wright Mills and the Power Elite* (Beacon Press, 1968).

bring together the class-rule and institutional-elite perspectives that are sometimes viewed as separate or even opposing approaches to the analysis of power. Then, too, the simultaneous consideration of ruling class and power elite, as I have defined them, allows us to deal with the everyday observation—which is also the first objection raised by critics of ruling-class theory— that some members of the ruling class are not involved in ruling, and that some of its leaders are not members of the class. Within the present framework, this objection is not a problem at all. There always have been members of ruling classes who have spent much of their time playing polo, riding to hounds or leading a world-wide social life. A ruling class is a privileged social class which is able to maintain its top position in the social structure, and there is no implication that each and every member of this social class must be involved in ruling, or that a person automatically falls from the class if he or she merely enjoys the disproportionate benefits that are appropriated by the ruling class. At the same time, there always have been carefully groomed and carefully selected employees from lower social classes whose advancement to important positions has been dependent upon their ability to solve problems and attain goals that are determined by the needs and desires of the ruling class.

However, not all upwardly mobile leaders in the United States are part of the power elite. As I have defined it, the power elite does not include labor leaders, even those appointed to government, for they are neither members of the social upper class nor employees of its institutions. Middle-American politicians elected to political office are not members of the power elite by this definition. Nor are leaders of minority group organizations. These examples are meant to emphasize that strata of the working class and specific social and ethnic groups have leaders too.

From a pluralistic point of view, the existence of these separate sources of leadership may be seen as evidence against the ruling-class view. From a class-hegemony view, however, the problem is not to deny that there are leaders from other classes or social groups, but to demonstrate how the ruling class, through the power elite, is able to impose its policies and ideologies in opposition to the leaders of various strata of the nonpropertied, wage-earning class. To include such people in a definition of the power elite would be to abandon any attempt to support empirically a class-based model of power in America.

With definitional problems clarified, it is possible to turn briefly to several criticisms of ruling-class theory that should be dealt with preliminary to a detailed consideration of the processes of domination. While these criticisms cannot be discussed here in a definitive way, it is possible to indicate the broad outlines of an answer to each of them, thus ensuring that peripheral questions do not detract from the main argument of later chapters.

The first argument against a ruling-class perspective is that the alleged ruling class is never specified in such a way that it can be studied empirically. I have tried to meet this objection by reputational, positional and statistical studies which show that certain social registers, blue books, private schools and social clubs are good—but by no means perfect—indicators of ruling-class standing.[26] Through the use of these sociological indicators, it is possible to do a wide variety of empirical studies of the ruling class, including studies of its socialization practices, its charitable involvements, its kinship networks and its historical continuity.

A second common objection is that there is no reason to believe that the alleged ruling class is "cohesive" enough to have the "will" and "class consciousness" to develop class-oriented policies and ideologies, much less to impress them upon the government and general public. This is an important argument, for most pluralists and Marxists have insisted upon social cohe-

26. G. William Domhoff, *The Higher Circles* (Random House, 1970), chapter 1.

siveness and in-group consciousness as part of their definitional criteria of a social class. In responding to this argument, I have tried to demonstrate the social cohesiveness of the American ruling class by presenting systematic evidence on interregional private school attendance, overlapping club memberships that are nationwide in scope, interlocking corporate directorships and nationwide attendance at annual retreats such as the Bohemian Grove and Rancheros Visitadores.[27] Others have provided evidence for social cohesion based upon intermarriage patterns, intermingling at summer and winter resorts, and clique patterns of a regional nature within the business community.[28]

While educational and social interactions are important evidence for the type of social cohesion from which class awareness can be inferred, it is also important to develop evidence of policy cohesion and a common ideology. Evidence for ruling-class cohesion at these levels also exists. It will be presented in later chapters as part of the argument concerning the policy-planning and ideology processes. For now it is enough to say that many of these common policies and ideologies are developed in specific ruling-class institutions and organizations like the Council on Foreign Relations, Committee for Economic Development, Business Council, Conference Board, Population Council and National Municipal League. These organizations, in turn, are linked with social clubs and corporations. Quantitative studies which systematically analyze the relationships among large numbers of corporations, social clubs and policy-planning groups are perhaps

27. Domhoff, *The Higher Circles, op. cit.*, chapters 2 and 4; G. William Domhoff, *The Bohemian Grove and Other Retreats* (Harper & Row, 1974).

28. Paul M. Blumberg and P. W. Paul, "Continuities and Discontinuities in Upper-Class Marriages," *Journal of Marriage and the Family*, February, 1975; Stephen Birmingham, *The Right Places* (Little, Brown and Co., 1968); and John Sonquist and Thomas Koenig, "Interlocking Directorates in the Top U.S. Corporations: A Graph Theory Approach," *The Insurgent Sociologist*, Spring, 1975.

most convincing in this regard. The overlaps and clique patterns found among organizations concerned with economic, social and policy matters suggest there is an institutional basis for the kind of generalized world view that is the very essence of class consciousness.[29]

There are many social scientists who would concede that a social upper class exists in the United States. Nonetheless, only a few of them also would agree that this class is a ruling class. One reason many resist this next step is that they believe the upper class no longer controls the banks and corporations that dominate the economy. According to this third objection to ruling-class theory, there has been a separation between the ownership and control of major corporations in the United States. The social upper class reaps the major benefits from large banks and corporations, as the statistics on stock ownership and wealth distribution make very clear, and many of its members sit on corporate boards of directors, but these huge enterprises are allegedly controlled by corporate managers of diverse social origins who remain somewhat separate from the ruling class and sometimes have more "public-regarding," less profit-oriented goals.[30]

29. G. William Domhoff, "Social Clubs, Policy-Planning Groups, and Corporations: A Network Study of Ruling-Class Cohesiveness," *The Insurgent Sociologist*, Spring, 1975; Philip Bonacich and G. William Domhoff, "Overlapping Memberships Among Clubs and Policy Groups of the American Ruling Class," paper presented at the annual meeting of The American Sociological Association, Chicago, 1977.

30. E.g., Talcott Parsons, "A Revised Analytical Approach to the Theory of Social Stratification," in Reinhard Bendix and Seymour M. Lipset, eds., *Class, Status, and Power* (Free Press, 1953), pp. 122–123; Bell, *op cit.*, chapter 2; and John K. Galbraith, *The New Industrial State*, second ed. (New American Library, 1971), p. xix. For other statements of this view, see the critical review article by Maurice Zeitlin, "Corporate Ownership and

The notion of a "managerial revolution" is difficult to refute fully and completely because of an absence of adequate information on corporate ownership and on the functioning of boards of directors. Indeed, the idea itself was able to take hold because its advocates accepted at face value the scanty information on corporate ownership available to them. Rather than assuming that the big rich continued to control corporations unless it was shown otherwise, they assumed from the little information corporations would release that wealthy people no longer controlled them. They then challenged their opponents to prove otherwise. It was a very unusual reversal of investigatory procedure, but the idea has had considerable staying power even in the face of evidence to the contrary. Thus, Robert A. Dahl could write in 1970 that it was a "resounding" and "incontrovertible fact" that ownership and control have been "split apart," even though a careful survey of some of the evidence six years earlier by a traditional social scientist, Earl Cheit, had concluded that "it is far from clear that attenuation of ownership control is as complete as is generally assumed."[31] Sociologist Maurice Zeitlin has chronicled numerous other examples of the persistence of the "pseudo-fact" of a managerial revolution in a detailed survey of the controversy which makes a powerful case for continuing dominance by corporate owners.[32]

The following kinds of evidence controvert the managerial revolution view and the resultant claim that America has been transformed from a class-based, exploitative economic system to a bureaucratic one in which class conflict is a thing of the past

---

Control: The Large Corporations and the Capitalist Class," *American Journal of Sociology*, 79, No. 5, 1974, pp. 1073–1119.

31. Robert A. Dahl, *After the Revolution?* (Yale Univ. Press, 1970), p. 125; Earl F. Cheit, "The New Place of Business," in Earl F. Cheit, ed., *The Business Establishment* (Wiley & Sons, 1964), p. 172.

32. Zeitlin, *op. cit.*

and everyone receives rewards in relation to the importance of his or her functional role in various institutional hierarchies:

1. A highly disproportionate number of bank and corporation directors are members of the ruling class according to our sociological criteria of social registers, private schools and social clubs.[33] This suggests that the general direction of these enterprises remains within the ruling class, for there is reason to believe that directors often play a significant role in the major issues that face a corporation. This is particularly the case when the corporation is in crisis, when a merger is being considered or a large-scale change in management is contemplated.[34]

2. There is good evidence for the argument that the highest-level managers of middle-class origins are assimilated into many of the social institutions of the ruling class as they take advantage of stock options and other devices which turn them into significant property owners in their own right. Top managers come to have a common class situation or class position with owners.[35]

3. There is evidence that the firms alleged to be managerially controlled are just as profit-oriented as owner-controlled firms, which deals with the claim that managers have different goals from ruling-class owners and directors.[36]

4. The most careful study of ownership records shows that many more companies are family- or owner-controlled than managerial revolution advocates have claimed.[37]

33. G. William Domhoff, *Who Rules America?* (Prentice-Hall, 1967), chapter 2.

34. *Ibid.*

35. Gabriel Kolko, *Wealth and Power in America* (Praeger, 1962); Zeitlin, *op. cit.*; Domhoff, *Who Rules America?*, *op. cit.*, chapter 2.

36. Zeitlin, *op. cit.*

37. Philip H. Burch, Jr., *The Managerial Revolution Reassessed* (Heath-Lexington, 1972).

5. There is evidence that in some industries the corporations are controlled in good measure through financial institutions that are clearly controlled by members of the ruling class.[38]

6. There is reason to believe that studies of the kinship networks, family offices and holding companies of major owning families would show they have much greater involvement in many companies than a superficial glance would indicate.[39]

The claim that ownership and control have been separated in large corporations has been a potent reason for ignoring ruling-class theory. However, by far the most important and longstanding criticism of this theory is that it does not provide adequate evidence for ruling-class domination of government. Closely related to this criticism is the assertion that an adequate ruling-class theory must show how the ruling class molds public opinion, for in the pluralist view it is ultimately public opinion, whether operating through voluntary associations or elections, which generally determines how government officials will act.

My first attempt to answer these kinds of criticisms was to show that members of the power elite hold a great many posi-

38. Zeitlin, op. cit.; Reuben Robertson, III, and Mimi Cutler, Testimony, in Corporate Disclosure, Part 1, Hearings Before the Senate Subcommittee on Intergovernmental Relations, 93rd Congress (U.S. Government Printing Office, 1974); Voting Rights in Major Corporations, a staff study prepared by the Subcommittee on Reports, Accounting and Management of the Committee on Government Affairs, United States Senate (U.S. Government Printing Office, 1978); David M. Kotz, Bank Control of Large Corporations in the United States (University of California Press, 1978).

39. Charles L. Schwartz and G. William Domhoff, "Probing the Rockefeller Fortune," Nomination of Nelson A. Rockefeller To Be Vice-President of the United States, Committee on the Judiciary, 93rd Congress (U.S. Government Printing Office, 1974); Marvin G. Dunn, "Kinship and Class: A Study of the Weyerhauser Family," unpublished Ph.D. dissertation, Univ. of Oregon, 1977.

tions in government and in opinion-molding institutions. The presence of such people is especially impressive in the Executive branch of the federal government.[40] But critics were not satisfied by this sociology-of-leadership or positional approach, which infers "power" to be operating when a disproportionate number of people from a class, ethnic group or racial group appear in positions of decision-making responsibility in a given institution or governmental branch. Although no social scientists question the findings of this method when it is used to show discrimination against subordinated groups on the part of banks, corporations, universities or the government, weaknesses are discovered in it when it is used to study the powerful instead of the powerless. In keeping with their process-oriented bias in the conceptualization of power indicators, the critics want to see the position holders in action, to see the various means and mechanisms by which they supposedly govern in the interests of the ruling class. Such critics often argue, as sociologist Arnold Rose did in a well-known pluralistic textbook, that members of the power elite may not act in the interests of the ruling class while in governmental positions; rather, they may act in terms of their conception of the national interest.[41] Such an argument forces us back to a consideration of process, for it makes it necessary to understand how "the national interest" is formulated and agreed upon.

However, it was not merely pluralists who were dissatisfied with positional indicators of power over government. Marxists influenced by the structuralist views of French Marxist-Leninist

40. Domhoff, *Who Rules America?*, *op. cit.*, chapters 3–6. For recent evidence on the President's cabinet and on Congress, see Beth Mintz, "The President's Cabinet, 1897–1972: A Contribution to the Power Structure Debate," *The Insurgent Sociologist*, Spring, 1975, and Richard Zweigenhaft, "Who Represents America?," *The Insurgent Sociologist*, Spring 1975.

41. Arnold M. Rose, *The Power Structure* (Oxford Univ. Press, 1967), pp. 23 and 93.

Nicos Poulantzas rejected this evidence because they can conceive of situations where a government could act in the interests of the ruling class without the ruling class having any members in it.[42] Indeed, Marxists such as Poulantzas sometimes argue that it is better for the capitalist system if ruling-class members are not part of the governmental apparatus, for capitalists are too divided among themselves and too short-sighted to formulate the general policies necessary for the prosperity of the overall system. Although this view shows a fundamental misunderstanding of the fact that positional overrepresentation was only being used by social scientists such as myself as one *indicator* of power, it does have to be taken seriously. Underlying it is a concern, similar to that of pluralists, with the processes through which the general interests of the ruling class are developed and through which these general interests are then allegedly furthered by the government.[43]

Processes of domination, and particularly of the federal government, will be the focus of the succeeding chapters of this book. As a background for that discussion, this chapter has presented an overview of the evidence which suggests that there is a small, relatively cohesive, clearly demarcated social upper class in the United States which has a disproportionate amount of the nation's privately held wealth and yearly income. It has argued that members of this class are intimately involved in major banks and corporations, if not as controllers of each and every one, then certainly as the major benefactors of them and as the directors

42. Nicos Poulantzas, "The Problem of the Capitalist State," *New Left Review*, no. 58, 1969; Nicos Poulantzas, *Political Power and Social Classes* (New Left Books, 1973).

43. For the most influential Marxist statement of the concern with the processes by which overall policies are developed, see Claus Offe, "Structural Problems of the Capitalist State," in Klaus von Beyme, ed., *German Political Studies* (Sage Publications, 1974).

who set their general policies. Moreover, it has suggested that members of this upper class, and high-level employees in banks, corporations, foundations and other institutions controlled by members of the upper class, are frequently found in positions of importance in government and in opinion-molding institutions. If this information on the existence of an upper class and the involvement of many of its members in positions of importance in corporations and government is taken as a starting point, the problem becomes one of untangling the processes by which the ruling class dominates the state apparatus in its own interests. The next chapter begins that task at the most basic and directly observable level.

2
The Special-Interest Process

Ruling-class domination of government can be seen most directly in the workings of lobbyists, backroom super-lawyers, trade associations and advisory committees to governmental departments and agencies. It takes place in a network of people and organizations that is knit together by varying combinations of information, gifts, bribes, insider dealing, friendship and, not least, promises of lucrative private jobs in the future for compliant government officials. This is the aspect of business-government relations described by journalists and social scientists in their exposés and case studies concerning regulatory agencies, congressional committees and Cabinet departments. It is the world that has been the target of the numerous investigations by Ralph Nader and his colleagues. This is the level of what I call the special-interest process; it consists of the several means by which individuals, families, corporations and business sectors within the ruling class obtain tax breaks, favors, subsidies and procedural rulings that are beneficial to their short-run interests.

The workings of the special-interest process are familiar to anyone who reads a newspaper regularly or has taken an introductory course in political science. Indeed, the process is so well known and so lucrative to the corporate rich that it is often taken as the sum and substance of governmental decision-making. Moreover, the strife and conflict that often erupts within this arena, occasionally pitting one business sector against another, reinforces a pluralistic image of power in America, including the image of a divided ruling class.

If the process itself is fairly obvious in its general outlines, most of the men and women who operate within it are neither well known nor prominent. They usually are not chairpersons of major corporations, partners in Wall Street law firms, presidents of large foundations or highly regarded research experts from major universities. Instead, they are lesser members of the power elite—corporate managers two or three rungs from the top, lawyers who have risen from middle-level backgrounds on the basis of their experience in specific government agencies and former politicians who have been hired by corporations or trade associations because of their connections. Of 124 registered lobbyists whose social backgrounds were investigated by one of my students in 1965, none were from the ruling class.[1]

The special-interest process can be studied from two different angles. One approach starts with a specific family, corporation, industry or trade association and follows its favor-seeking operations through the particular combination of congressional committees, regulatory agencies and executive bureaucracies that must be wired in order to gain the desired governmental action. The second starts with the functioning of a given regulatory agency, congressional committee, executive department or advisory committee in order to determine how various special inter-

1. Douglas Eddy, "The Lobbyists," as noted in G. William Domhoff, *Who Rules America?* (Prentice-Hall, 1967), p. 171.

ests impinge upon it. Sometimes the investigator has planned the study in advance, but just as often he or she is taking advantage of an accident, scandal or leak that promises to shed new knowledge on machinations which cost the general public tens of billions of dollars each year.

There are innumerable case studies of the special-interest process, most of which are summarized in popular books by journalists and textbooks by political scientists.[2] They are so numerous and easily accessible that only selected examples need be provided. These examples will make the nature of the special-interest process abundantly clear. Equally important, the examples will provide a basis for understanding why most social scientists do not accept these kinds of studies as sufficient evidence for the assertion that a ruling class dominates government in the United States.

OBTAINING TAX BREAKS

The ways in which wealthy families and their corporations obtain tax breaks provides a good entry point into the special-interest process, for the mechanisms are several and the rewards are very great. The most famous tax-break case of the past thirty years involved the billionaire Du Pont family of Delaware and a Washington lawyer. In 1961 the Justice Department succeeded in convincing the Supreme Court to break Du Pont family control of both General Motors and the Du Pont Corporation in a court

2. E.g., Douglas Cater, *Power in Washington* (Random House, 1964); Drew Pearson and Jack Anderson, *The Case Against Congress* (Simon and Schuster, 1968); Robert Sherrill, *Why They Call It Politics* (Harcourt, 1972); Morton Mintz and Jerry S. Cohen, *America, Inc.* (Dial Press, 1971); Morton Mintz and Jerry S. Cohen, *Power, Inc.* (Viking Press, 1976); and Michael Parenti, *Democracy for the Few*, second ed. (St. Martin's Press, 1977).

case that had been dragging on since 1949. The Court ruled that Du Pont Corporation and the family holding company, Christiana Securities, would have to sell their GM stock. Leaders within the family decided to sell the stock to individual members of the family. This assured that the family's potential influence would lurk in the background of GM decision-making. But there remained the problem of paying taxes on the profits made from selling the stock.

In order to avoid or greatly reduce the tax, the family hired Washington lawyer Clark Clifford, who had made his mark as a Democratic advisor to President Harry Truman before developing a lucrative private practice based upon corporate clients. Clifford and his aides decided that the Du Pont problem required special legislation. They wrote a bill which would allow the Du Ponts to pay the tax on the profits at the maximum capital-gains rate of 25 percent rather than at ordinary income tax rates. According to one estimate by the Treasury Department, this reduced the tax liability from $45 per share to $7.25 per share.[3] To assure passage of the bill, Clifford and others arranged for a family spokesperson, Crawford Greenwalt, president of Du Pont Corporation, to meet with every member of the Senate Finance Committee and the House Ways and Means Committee. This personal lobbying, along with the efforts of the Democratic senator from the Du Ponts' home state of Delaware, led to the passage of the bill. For his help and advice, Clifford was paid $1 million over a ten-year period in yearly "retainer fees" of $100,000.[4]

Special tax legislation usually does not require such elaborate lobbying and large retainer fees. More often it is quietly tacked

3. Joseph Goulden, *The Superlawyers* (Weybright & Talley, 1971), pp. 94–96. For another account, see Gerald C. Zilg, *Du Pont: Behind the Nylon Curtain* (Prentice-Hall, 1974), p. 394ff.

4. Goulden, *op. cit.*, p. 96.

on to one or another piece of general tax legislation by a single legislator or a staff aide. One of the major complaints by liberal senators about Colin F. Stam, who served as Chief of Staff of the Joint Committee on Internal Revenue Taxation from 1938 to 1964, concerned "his role in drafting and defending narrow tax provisions which helped particular industries, companies, or in the case of Louis B. Mayer, one individual."[5]

Sometimes the criticisms of tax breaks by liberals are turned against them, thereby revealing that legislators of all political persuasions are involved in the special-interest process. Southern conservative Russell Long (D.-La.) demonstrated this rather nicely in the case of liberal Senator Walter Mondale (D.-Minn.) shortly after Mondale received the vice presidential nomination. Long was annoyed that liberals were criticizing his Finance Committee's tax-reform bill for providing even more loopholes for special interests. So he gave his committee a second chance to vote on provisions of the bill—in full view of the public. As *Business Week* warned shortly before this second meeting, "Long's extraordinary action could prove embarrassing to some members of the Senate who have been leading the fight for tax reform against Long." This was because "several of the costly special-interest provisions of Long's bill were sponsored by 'reformers.' "[6]

The open session did prove mildly embarrassing to some people, including Mondale. Eleven amendments that had been

5. John F. Manley, "Congressional Staff and Public Policy-Making: The Joint Committee on Internal Revenue Taxation," *Journal of Politics*, November, 1958, as reprinted in Theodore J. Lowi and Randall B. Ripley, *Legislative Politics USA* (Little, Brown, 1973), p. 351.

Louis B. Mayer was a founder of MGM who saved $2 million in taxes when he retired by hiring a Washington lawyer to lobby through a special tax provision that applied only to him. For a good treatment of special tax legislation for individuals, see Philip M. Stern, *The Rape of the Taxpayer* (Random House, 1973), chapter 3.

6. "Long's tax-reform ploy," *Business Week*, July 19, 1976, p. 28.

criticized as gross favoritism were removed from the legislation, and five others were scaled down, for a total saving to the Treasury of about $175 million a year. Such companies as Sun Oil, Superior Oil, Cargill, Tenneco, Freeport Minerals, Hanna Mining, Texas Optical and Encyclopaedia Britannica had their amendments eliminated. However, by far the most interesting of the amendments eliminated were those by vice presidential nominee Mondale, who discreetly absented himself from the open meeting:

Among the amendments dropped by the committee were two sponsored by Senator Mondale, the Democratic vice presidential nominee, in an effort to benefit two firms in his home state of Minnesota. Mondale, a member of the Finance Committee, did not attend the meeting yesterday and no one spoke up for his proposals.

One would have allowed a special tax credit for homeowners who install clock thermostats to conserve energy. A major manufacturer of the devices is Honeywell, Inc. The primary beneficiary of the second Mondale amendment would have been the Minnesota-based Investors Diversified Services. The aim of the amendment, which would have cost the Treasury $250,000 a year, was to defer payment of taxes on interest from "face-amount certificates" issued by the investors syndicate.[7]

Mondale may have been personally embarrassed by the revelations of his friendly service to major corporations. However, he was not hurt politically by the stories, for they are commonplace and generally accepted unless there is a hint of outright bribe or payoff. Potentially more disastrous for the politicians involved was the discovery in 1975 of campaign donations by multimillionaire H. Ross Perot to twelve members of the House Ways

7. Associated Press, "Senate OKs Tax Changes," San Francisco *Chronicle*, July 24, 1976, p. 5.

and Means Committee shortly before the introduction to the full House of a special tax amendment that would have benefited Perot greatly. Written by Sheldon S. Cohen, a Washington lawyer who had been Internal Revenue Service Commissioner during the Johnson administration, the amendment could have saved Perot an estimated $15 million. Although the amendment had been voted by Ways and Means, with ten of the twelve who had received money from Perot voting for it, it fell by the wayside when the story of the contributions broke in the *Wall Street Journal.* All ten Congressmen denied any knowledge that the bill would have benefited Perot, and Perot denied that he had inspired the amendment. There the matter was dropped.[8]

There are other avenues into tax breaks, including direct contact with the Treasury Department and indirect pressure through one or another of the President's special aides. Enough has been said, however, to show that the process works to the benefit of those who can afford expensive lawyers or who have direct access to government officials and their staffs. At the same time, the very fact that some of these examples exist shows that the special interests are sometimes thwarted by investigative journalists or by minor political conflicts among legislators. The special interests only win most of the time on tax favors.[9]

THWARTING THE REGULATORY AGENCIES

It is a commonplace that regulatory agencies are often controlled by the businesses they are supposed to regulate. Just about every

8. Mintz and Cohen, *Power, Inc., op. cit.* pp. 592–593.

9. The full story of tax breaks has been masterfully presented by Stern, *op. cit.* For a brief academic account of the major factors leading to tax breaks, see Stanley S. Surrey, "How Special Tax Provisions Get Enacted," in Lowi and Ripley, *op. cit.*

study acknowledges or demonstrates that point.[10] Nor are the mechanisms of this dominance unfamiliar. Many of the agency leaders come directly from the regulated industry. Conversely, longtime agency employees often leave to work for a law firm which represents clients before the agency, or for businesses supposedly being regulated by it. The studies also provide other reasons—the agencies are understaffed, they are harassed by congressional committees that look out for the special interests, they are influenced by lobbyists, and information is withheld from them by the businesses themselves.

Anthropologist David L. Serber conducted one of the best studies of a regulatory agency at the state level in Pennsylvania. He spent several months between December, 1973 and March, 1974 listening and observing among both agency personnel and industry lobbyists. His study is especially informative because it shows the nature of industry control—in this case, the insurance industry—even in the face of an agency director who had made his reputation as a critic of insurance companies and was determined to make them more responsive to consumers.[11]

The reformer in question was Herbert L. Dennenberg, a professor at the Wharton School of Finance, University of Pennsylvania, who had written numerous articles highly critical of the functioning of insurance companies. He was appointed to head the insurance regulatory agency in 1971 by Democratic Governor Milton Shapp, much to the displeasure of the insurance leaders, who were used to suggesting new agency directors. Upon taking office, Dennenberg announced his intentions to reform the regu-

10. E.g., Bernard Schwartz, *The Professor and the Commissions* (Knopf, 1959); Robert Fellmeth, *The Interstate Commerce Omission* (Grossman, 1970); James Turner, *The Chemical Feast* (Grossman, 1970); and Mark J. Green, ed., *The Monopoly Makers* (Grossman, 1973).

11. David L. Serber, "Regulating Reform: The Social Organization of Insurance Regulation," *The Insurgent Sociologist*, Spring, 1975.

latory system and turn the Department of Insurance into a consumer-oriented agency. The motto of the agency became "the consumer has been screwed long enough."

Dennenberg began with a flurry, including public castigation of various insurance company practices, thereby further raising the ire of his opponents. He published a series of pamphlets that were to serve as "shoppers' guides" to insurance. He formalized procedures that had become informal. He utilized state codes that allowed him to hold disciplinary proceedings against companies, and he hired new non-civil–service staff who had no links to the insurance industry or the political parties. He also brought about several minor reforms, but that was all. His hands were tied because the industry had so many different means by which it could thwart leadership it did not like.

First, the industry had access to the entire bureaucracy because numerous members of both staff and management were former insurance company employees. Serber notes that "It is common for an individual to retire early from an insurance company and collect his pension while working for the Pennsylvania Department of Insurance."[12] Of 67 people working at the staff level of the department office in the state capitol, 58 had a background in the insurance industry. At the managerial level, 10 of the top 12 offices were filled by men from the insurance industry.

Second, the industry stayed in constant contact with department staff and management through a large lobbying operation. In particular, most insurance companies in the state, including the largest, are part of the Insurance Federation of Pennsylvania, which employs a highly paid lobbyist, an attorney, two public relations specialists and a support staff to interact with the insurance department. In addition, the federation has three standing committees of company executives which meet regularly with the federation employees to plan strategy and set priorities.

12. *Ibid.*, p. 86.

Federation employees and executives of member companies are in communication with department personnel through luncheons and visits. They try to interact in a cordial and respectful manner, building up a friendly relationship rather than an authoritarian or adversarial one. Both executives and lobbyists give gifts to department personnel, particularly at Christmastime, thereby helping to develop a deeper bond and perhaps a feeling of obligation on the part of the employees.[13]

However, the relationships between department employees and industry representatives are not merely social in the usual sense of the term. They also involve constant informal interaction over new regulations and problems of possible rule violations. Indeed, the fact that so many problems are handled in this informal manner leads Serber to emphasize that "the regulatory process at this level, theoretically the most technical and objective level of regulation, is a social process."[14]

The insurance lobbyists also have developed an intimate tie with important state legislators. This provides the industry with leverage on the insurance department, for the legislature must approve the commissioners appointed by the governor, set the budget and provide the legislative guidelines within which the department functions. These ties to the legislature are of two types—insurance people who become legislators, and lobbyists who interact with legislators. Serber found that several legislators on committees dealing with the insurance industry had relationships with the industry, either as former employees, directors of newly formed insurance agencies, or as lawyers in law firms with major insurance clients. On the other side of the coin, insurance

13. For an unsurpassed account of gift exchanges all over the world, see Marcel Mauss, *The Gift* (Free Press, 1954). The psychological potency of gift-giving is often overlooked in the rationalistic literature of modern-day political science and political sociology.

14. Serber, *op. cit.*, p. 92.

lobbyists and executives were regular campaign contributors to legislators, directly and indirectly, and provided them with numerous gifts and free transportation. Through informants and direct observation, Serber learned that lobbyists attended legislative committee meetings and took a large role in drafting legislation.

The net result of these multilevel linkages was that the insurance industry was by and large able to block Dennenberg's reform efforts. Their informal meetings with entrenched bureaucrats increased despite Dennenberg's wishes to the contrary. The staff gave him and his aides considerable internal resistance to his new initiatives. An attempt to formally regulate gift-giving was a failure:

At one point, rather late in the reform administration, a formal regulation was proposed and drafted which would have prohibited Department employees from accepting gifts and luncheons from industry representatives. Staff would be required to report all such offers of gifts to the Commissioner. . . . The proposal was sent to each bureau of the Department to determine the responses of the staff. All civil service staff including the Deputy Commissioner argued against the regulation as being impractical, counterproductive, impossible to enforce, and/or an invasion of privacy. The proposal encountered such resistance from the civil service staff that it had to be abandoned.[15]

The industry also made it clear to department personnel that it would outlast Dennenberg. Its representatives warned that he would be out of office before the next election. They also promised good jobs in insurance companies to department personnel who were loyal to them, and they made good on their promise:

In four out of five cases, civil service staff leaving the Dennenberg administration, who did not retire, were given industry jobs directly linked to their activities as regulators, as had been promised. Even

15. *Ibid.*, p. 99.

some of Dennenberg's appointees were enticed to leave the agency to accept jobs in the industry. For example, one of his first communications assistants left to take over the public relations job for the Insurance Federation of Pennsylvania.[16]

Along with its efforts within the department, which were highly successful in hampering Dennenberg's reforms, the insurance lobby intensified its pressure on the legislature, generating a bipartisan opposition to his administration. Over a three-year period, "not a single piece of legislation sponsored by the Department of Insurance and opposed by the large lobby association was passed."[17] Furthermore, leading legislators publicly called for Dennenberg's resignation, and claimed that the legislature would not approve his reappointment after the next election.

Dennenberg resigned his post in March, 1974, seven months before his term was to expire. He did so to seek the Democratic nomination for United States Senate, a nomination which he lost by a few thousand votes in a close primary race. He was replaced at the department by a man whom the insurance companies had suggested would be acceptable. Relations between the industry and the department returned to normal at all levels.

There are instances where regulatory agencies have acted in the public interest on one or another specific issue, although this is often only because a morally angry or personally by-passed employee has taken a public stand or leaked information that led to publicity or scandal. However, such instances are few and far between, and significant reform attempts such as Dennenberg's are even more rare. The situation for most regulatory agencies could be characterized by this summary of the activities of the Interstate Commerce Commission:

16. *Ibid.*
17. *Ibid.*, p. 100.

The ICC, once run by the railroads, has modernized in the last few decades by selling out to the truckers. It is now in the business of keeping truck rates even higher to prevent them from competing. As a sideline, the ICC publishes a tough truck-safety code, which it does not enforce, and weak household-movers' code, which it also does not enforce.[18]

Regulatory agencies, then, are tightly enmeshed in the special-interest network.

SELF-SERVING ADVICE TO THE BUREAUCRACY

The hundreds of advisory committees that oversee the functioning of government agencies were as little known as the regulatory agencies are well known until Senator Lee Metcalf (D -Mont.) and the executive secretary of his staff, Vic Reinemer, turned their attention to them in the early 1970's. The result was a series of hearings and changes in the law which have publicized another method by which dozens of special interests shape governmental functioning in the areas of interest to them.[19] Senator Metcalf's investigations, and the yearly reports which are mandated by new

18. Sherrill, *op. cit.*, p. 181, quoting law professor Leonard Ross.

19. *Advisory Committees*, Hearings Before the Subcommittee on Intergovernmental Relations of the Committee on Government Operations, United States Senate, 91st Congress, 2nd Session, and 92nd Congress, 1st Session (U.S. Government Printing Office, 1970, 1971); Vic Reinemer, "Budget Bureau: Do Advisory Panels Have an Industry Bias?" *Science*, July 3, 1970; Vic Reinemer, "Corporate Government in Action," *Progressive*, November, 1971; Kit Gage and Samuel S. Epstein, "The Federal Advisory Committee System: An Assessment," *Environmental Law Reporter*, February, 1977.

legislation passed in 1972, reveal that there are between 1,000 and 1,500 advisory committees at work in the federal government in any given year. Many of these are committees of scientists, technicians and academicians who help evaluate government programs and select recipients of research grants and contracts. Others are advisory committees on monuments, commemorations and celebrations which seem to have a rather perfunctory and symbolic role. The remainder are business advisory committees dominated by people from the industry affected by the given agency.[20] Thus, oil executives preponderate on the National Petroleum Council, and major corporate polluters made up the National Industrial Pollution Control Council, which had considerable success in hampering vigorous enforcement of the environmental protection laws during its six years of existence.[21]

There are numerous examples of how the advisory committee mechanism operates within the special-interest process. One of the most surprising involves the way the Advisory Council on Federal Reports, which works with the Office of Management and Budget, is able to shape the information flow into executive departments and regulatory agencies. The Advisory Council on Federal Reports was established in 1942 in response to a law which stipulated that there should be greater coordination in the collection of information from industry. Funded by private industry and staffed by employees and officers of large trade associations like the Chamber of Commerce and the National Association

20. See Henry J. Steck, "Power and the Policy Process: Advisory Committees in the Federal Government," paper delivered to the annual meeting of the American Political Science Association, Washington, D.C., 1972, pp. 5–9, for a categorization of the types of committees.

21. Henry J. Steck, "Private Influence on Environmental Policy: The Case of the National Industrial Pollution Control Council," *Environmental Law*, Winter, 1975.

of Manufacturers, the council sets up subcommittees to review requests for information by government officials. In exercising its powers the council has stopped questionnaires from being sent, changed their wording or eliminated certain questions. Several attempts to gather information for pollution control were blocked or delayed through this device. Other information was denied as well:

In 1963 the Federal Trade Commission submitted to the Budget Bureau a questionnaire designed to obtain information on ownership and interlocks of the nation's 1,000 leading corporations. The advisory committees strongly objected, then carried their inside information to Capitol Hill, where they obtained prohibition of expenditures on the survey. Electric and gas utilities used the advisory committees to weaken Federal Power Commission attempts to obtain more information on utilities' expenditures for professional services, including payment made to law firms, advertising, public relations, and lobbying.[22]

The functioning of a special advisory committee to the Defense Department has been subjected to detailed investigation through an examination by Diana Roose of ten years of its committee minutes, covering the years 1962 to 1972.[23] This study shows how important—and self-serving—the more active of these committees can be. The Industrial Advisory Council of the Department of Defense was established in 1962 by then-Secretary of Defense Robert McNamara, a former president of Ford Motor Company, because it was easier to have an advisory group than to deal with defense industry trade associations on "so many

22. Reinemer, "Budget Bureau: Do Advisory Panels Have an Industry Bias?" *op. cit.*, p. 37.
23. Diana Roose, "Top Dogs and Top Brass: An Inside Look at a Government Advisory Committee," *The Insurgent Sociologist*, Spring, 1975.

divergent problems."[24] The purpose of the council, called the IAC for short, was to provide a forum wherein military leaders and defense industry executives could iron out any problems in the process of providing weapons and equipment to the military. That is, it was primarily a logistics, rather than a policy-making, committee. A former Pentagon cost analyst, A. Ernest Fitzgerald, who was fired from his position in 1969 for exposing cost overruns, called the IAC "the board of directors of the military-industrial complex."[25]

The Industrial Advisory Council consisted of about twenty-five high-level executives from major businesses, most of them defense firms doing a large amount of business with the government. Top military brass and civilian leaders of the Defense Department also attended meetings, which were held three times a year at the Pentagon. Among the companies represented by their presidents or chairpersons were AT&T, Boeing, General Dynamics, Hughes Aircraft, Lockheed, Northrop, Rockwell International and Texas Instruments. In 1972 nine of the top fifteen defense contractors were members.

To find out what went on at the meetings, Roose catalogued the content of the IAC minutes into several categories. First, she found that over 50 percent of the agenda items concerned the mechanisms for ensuring the smooth flow of funds from government to industry. The council reviewed rules on the amortization of defense industry equipment, squabbled over "unallowable costs" and suggested changes in the regulations on both auditing

24. *Ibid.*, p. 62.

25. *Ibid.*, p. 55. Fitzgerald made this statement in a personal interview with Roose on June 14, 1972. For a firsthand description of the waste and corruption—i.e., extra executive salaries and company profits—in military procurement, see A. Ernest Fitzgerald, *The High Priests of Waste* (Norton, 1972).

and patent rights. In 1963 an IAC subcommittee recommended a "realistic profit policy" for noncompetitive military contracts. These new guidelines, once adopted by the Defense Department, pushed profit rates on negotiated contracts from 7.7 percent to 9.4 percent.[26]

A second major aspect of IAC work concerned broader policy issues in the manufacture and sale of weapons. When Pentagon officials suggested in 1968 that there should be a new profit policy based upon the amount of capital actually invested by defense industries, rather than on a percentage of their sales, council members were strongly opposed: "A heated discussion erupted with some members of the Council threatening to go to the highest level—apparently to the President himself—if there was any attempt to adopt this plan placing profit substantially on contractor investment."[27] The Pentagon backed down. However, when Congress ordered the General Accounting Office to do a study of defense industry profits in 1970, it was found that profits on the contracts studied were 56 percent of invested capital, compared with only 6.9 percent of sales. The Defense Department then slowly moved to a formula that was based to some degree on capital investment, which represented a partial defeat for the IAC on this specific question.

Another policy issue of concern to IAC members involved the export sales of military hardware. The council developed policies to further this aim in the middle of the 1960's, helping to boost the overseas sales of the defense industry from $1 billion in 1961 to over $6 billion in 1965 by using the Pentagon as its marketing arm. The council made another push for greater exports in the early 1970's, when the war in Southeast Asia was failing and their industries were suffering cutbacks in military contracts.

26. *Ibid.*, pp. 55–56.
27. *Ibid.*, p. 57.

This renewed effort followed in the wake of the Nixon administration's efforts to pressure American allies into assuming a greater
role in their defense against communist and socialist insurgencies
in the Third World and within their own countries. During this
period discussion within the council turned to such matters as
overseas pricing policies and plans to obtain more financial credits
from Congress for foreign military sales. Between 1970 and 1974
military sales increased by a factor of eight.[28]

The third and final facet of IAC meetings was the presentation of the administration's point of view on the war in Southeast
Asia. The business leaders were treated to briefings by top officials of the Johnson and Nixon administrations, followed by
question-and-answer periods.

Despite the importance of the IAC, it was disbanded in early
1974. The Department of Defense reacted very strongly to the
provisions for open meetings and public availability of meeting
records in the 1972 Federal Advisory Committee Act sponsored
by Senator Metcalf and others. As a Pentagon spokesperson
warned Senator Metcalf at the 1971 hearings, "I am inclined to
believe that if we were to move in the direction that you are
suggesting, we would be well advised to consider the logic of
even continuing the Industry Advisory Council."[29] That the meetings of the Industrial Advisory Council only would be useful if
they were strictly off the record is made clear by Roose's analysis
of the ten years of secret minutes that she obtained from an
anonymous source.

However, the dissolution of the IAC did not mean an end to
intimate industry/Defense Department contact. "We can still in-

28. Michael T. Klare, "The Political Economy of Arms Sales," *Society*,
September–October, 1974, provides an analysis of all the factors leading to
expanded arms sales abroad.

29. Roose, *op. cit.*, p. 61.

vite a group of businesspeople for lunch as long as they aren't the same people every time," the former executive secretary of the IAC told Roose.[30] Nor does the law prohibit the use of businesspeople as consultants. More generally, trade associations have resumed their former role as informal liaisons:

At the Pentagon, industry trade associations now do IAC's former work on matters of procurement and management policies. These lobbying associations represent specific groups of military industries, such as the Aerospace Industries Association or the National Security Industries Association. Through these longstanding associations, industry executives and their staffs work closely with the military on a daily basis, preparing reports and making recommendations about the business side of the Pentagon.[31]

Although the Defense Department felt the need for private meetings, most departments have continued with their advisory committees under the new law. The committees are more open to scrutiny and somewhat more representative in their membership, but they are still functioning, with thousands of trade associations, corporations and individual businesspeople taking part. To take the most dramatic examples for 1975, AT&T had 130 positions on advisory committees, RCA had 105, General Electric 74, Rockwell International 57 and ITT 53.[32] Although industrial advisory committees are no longer a "secret branch" of government or an "invisible bureaucracy," they are still a part of the process by which many business sectors protect or enhance their narrow interests.

30. *Ibid.*, pp. 61–62.

31. *Ibid.*

32. "New Index Shows Personnel and Corporate Influence on Federal Advisory Committees," *Congressional Record, Senate,* September 28, 1976, volume 22, no. 148, part II.

LOBBYING CONGRESSIONAL COMMITTEES

It is hardly news to say that committees do much of the work of Congress and state legislatures. The committees—and in some cases subcommittees—are the petty baronies of top legislative leaders.[33] Although congressional committees seldom initiate policy on large general issues, they are important on hundreds of narrow issues that in their totality add up to a great deal for the parties concerned. Not surprisingly, then, those who are affected by the actions of one or another committee usually work hand in hand with it on the issues that concern them. For example, agribusiness people keep an eye on the agricultural committees, the AFL-CIO and the National Education Association interact with the labor and education committees, and the banking and real estate interests birddog the money committees.[34]

The money committees of Congress are the Senate Banking, Housing and Urban Affairs Committee and the House Banking, Finance and Urban Affairs Committee. They deal with questions concerning the structure of the banking system, the financing of housing, the policies of urban renewal and the oversight of banking and currency regulatory agencies. A detailed study of these two committees by the Ralph Nader Congress Project provides a close look at the role of Congress and its committees in the special-interest process.[35]

To begin with, the banking committees have numerous members who are involved in the banking or housing business, or are

33. Woodrow Wilson, *Congressional Government* (Houghton Mifflin Co., 1885), p. 92; Cater, *op. cit.*, chapter 9; Mark Green, James M. Fallows and David R. Zwick, *Who Runs Congress?* (Bantam Books, 1972), chapter 3.

34. Pearson and Anderson, *op. cit.*, chapters 6 and 8; Richard F. Fenno, Jr., *Congressmen in Committees* (Little, Brown and Co., 1973), pp. 31–35.

35. Lester M. Salamon, *The Money Committees* (Grossman, 1975).

part of law firms whose clients are in one of those businesses.[36] They provide a basis from which these special interests can develop access to the committee. But even without this built-in starting point, banking and housing firms would have a strong relationship with the committee, for its members are befriended, advised and supported financially by several large trade associations—in particular, the American Bankers Association, the National Association of Home Builders and the U.S. Savings and Loan League. These organizations have a great impact on the committee in a variety of ways. In the case of the American Bankers Association:

The ABA maintains a research staff of several dozen to keep several steps ahead of information-starved congressional committees, a "government liaison" staff to present industry positions to Congressmen and keep track of committee activity, and a "contact-banker" system to bring the all-important local pressure to bear when it is needed."[37]

The efforts of the ABA and other lobbying organizations combine with the social and financial interests of the less-involved congressional members to sway those with no direct interest in banking and housing to adopt the industry point of view. A swing group of liberal Democrats and moderate Republicans on the House committee often goes along with what the vested interests desire for the kinds of reasons suggested by an insider who preferred to remain anonymous:

These guys come to Congress in their thirties as promising $20,000-$25,000-a-year-attorneys and businesspeople, with high ideals and great enthusiasm. But after six or seven years they find themselves approaching middle age with decent incomes but no real security, while their former law partners back home are secure and prosperous.

36. Salamon, *op. cit.*, p. 49; Pearson and Anderson, *op. cit.*
37. Salamon, *op. cit.*, p. 23.

They need $50,000-$150,000 to cover campaign costs every two years, just to stay in office. Since bank funds are easy to get, since bank issues are complex and therefore easy to camouflage, and since these members are socially close to the middle-level business-professional leadership of their communities in which local bankers play so crucial a role, support for banker positions on the committee comes to seem entirely natural.[38]

Given the direct and indirect linkages which banking and housing interests have to the committee, they seldom lost on an issue even when it was chaired by anti-banking populist Wright Patman between 1963 and 1974. Like many committee chairs, Patman was powerful because he had wide discretion in the employment of staff, in the shaping of subcommittees, in scheduling consideration of bills and in holding hearings. Because of these several powers, he was able to conduct studies of banking concentration that are invaluable to scholars, to block the banking interests from obtaining all they desired, and to introduce legislation that was deeply resented by the banking fraternity. Nonetheless, Patman could not win on the most important issues:

When it comes to the bank-regulation issues he cares most about, however, Patman's effectiveness has been much more limited. . . . Patman's efforts have not yet succeeded in disrupting the power of bank trust departments, in preventing interlocking directorates among banks or between them and other firms, in putting an end to bank ownership of stock in competing banks, in forcing banks and pension funds to invest a larger portion of their assets in housing or a National Development Bank, in bringing the Federal Reserve under greater congressional control or even in subjecting the Federal Reserve System to a General Accounting Office audit.[39]

38. *Ibid.*, p. 53.
39. *Ibid.*, p. 46.

The bankers could beat Patman, for all his seniority and chair power, because of their ties to other committee members, their even greater ties to the compliant Senate banking committee, their connections in the executive branch and their dominance of the Federal Reserve System. The conflict over a change in the banking laws in 1970–71 nicely demonstrates most of these points.

In 1968 major banks began to reconstitute themselves as part of "one-bank holding companies," meaning that they were now the only bank owned by a holding company that had the right to own nonbanking businesses as well. This legal maneuver made it possible for large banks to purchase and operate other businesses—equipment leasing, data processing, insurance and travel agencies. Although laws reaching back to the Depression years of the 1930's had built a barrier between commercial banking and other economic activities in order to ensure bank stability and greater economic competition, the 1956 Bank Holding Company Act had left one-bank holding companies unregulated because they seemed to be no threat at the time. By the late 1960's, however, the booming economy had produced large profits and deposits that banks were eager to invest, and the fears bred by banking practices in the Roaring Twenties were a thing of the past, at least in the bankers' minds.

By early 1969, 34 of the 100 largest banks had been reorganized as part of one-bank holding companies. In all, there were over 650 one-bank holding companies, and most of those owned other businesses that varied from insurance companies to manufacturing firms to farms. One-bank holding companies became a topic of discussion in the press and among liberal politicians, and they were criticized by the small businesspeople who stood to be hurt by bank expansion into their service-oriented activities. The need to do something about this phenomenon became apparent.

The focal point for those seeking new legislation to close the one-bank loophole became Wright Patman and his staff. They soon drafted a tough set of amendments and scheduled hearings on them. The amendments would close several loopholes in the 1956 Bank Holding Act, and restrict bank holding companies to ownership of businesses closely related to banking.[40] Several small-business groups supported the Patman bill. In addition, an organization of small bankers from forty states, the Independent Bankers Association, supported changes in the law.[41]

Shortly after Patman introduced his bill in February 1969, the Nixon administration came forward with a "reform" bill of its own to deal with the problem. It was written by Undersecretary of the Treasury Charls E. Walker, who had been the chief executive officer of the American Bankers Association before joining the government. This bill was significantly weaker than the Patman bill in almost every respect, but it did claim to close the loophole which the President said could not be left unchecked because the trend toward the combination of banking and business "would be bad for banking, bad for business, and bad for borrowers and consumers."[42]

At first the largest banks opposed any regulation of one-bank holding companies. However, opposition by smaller banks, and the strength of the attack by other small businesspeople and Patman, convinced them that some regulation was inevitable. They decided to work for the weakest legislation possible, with the amendments suggested by their former employee now in the Treasury Department as an acceptable fall-back position.

The bankers made their boldest move following the Patman committee's hearings on the issue. A Republican member of the committee drafted a one-page bill incorporating all of the suggestions of the American Bankers Association and offered it as a substitute for the Patman amendments. In addition to direct

40. *Ibid.*, pp. 115–116.
41. *Ibid.*, p. 121.
42. *Ibid.*, p. 116.

lobbying by the ABA employees in Washington, the association contacted the local bankers who had been assigned to each committee member, urging them to get in touch with their congressman and ask for support of the ABA position. The substitute measure replaced the tougher Patman bill by a 20–15 vote, thanks to a solid conservative bloc of Southern Democrats and Republicans.[43]

Not to be outdone, the Patman forces fought back on the floor of the House with the help of muckraking columns by Jack Anderson and lobbying by the National Association of Insurance Agents. They were able to portray the issue as one of "selling out to the banks," and House members were hesitant to be branded on such a controversial issue. The result was that the House passed a greatly strengthened bill which corresponded to the original Patman bill. The ABA had suffered a severe setback.

Defeated in the House because it had overstepped itself with a bill that was too blatantly favorable to big banks, the ABA turned its attention to the Senate, where its lobbyists were former banking committee staff members who had great access to its leadership. In addition, a former aide to committee chairman John Sparkman (D.-Ala.) was hired as a lobbyist for the bill by a large financial conglomerate, CIT Corporation.

It soon became clear that the new ABA strategy was one of delay, for Sparkman held off on Senate hearings. During this lull, the administration announced its intention to appoint a special blue-ribbon Commission on Financial Structure and Regulation to look into one-bank holding companies and related banking matters. Once again, it was former ABA officer Walker who took the lead in devising the administration position.[44]

---

43. *Ibid.*, p. 125.

44. When Walker left the Treasury after five years of service, he became one of the most sought-after lobbyists in Washington, representing fourteen major corporations with combined sales of $76 billion, and increasing his

But the strategy of delay did not work. The smaller business-people continued their pressure, and Patman retaliated against Sparkman by refusing to schedule hearings on a mass transit bill the Senate had passed. Thus, six months after the House passed its amended bill, the Senate Banking, Housing and Urban Affairs Committee began hearings. After twelve days of hearings which were dominated by spokespersons friendly to the big banks, the committee went into executive session, where it prepared a bill that was patterned after suggestions provided by ABA and other big-bank lobbyists with direct access to the committee.[45]

The smaller bankers and other small-business groups were once again prepared to oppose committee-proposed legislation. However, they had no success in lobbying the Senate. After several fights over critical amendments were lost by close votes, the ABA version of the bill passed by a 77–1 vote. Two very different versions of the bill therefore went to the House-Senate Conference Committee, which was charged with working out a satisfactory compromise.

Conference committees are one of the most important and least-known aspects of the legislative process. They also are one of the places where special interests are able to do the most benefit for themselves. Former Senator Albert Gore (D.-Tenn.) summarized his experience of conference committees as follows:

It is here, in secret meetings often not even announced until the last minute, that a few men can sit down and undo in one hour the most painstaking work of months of effort by several standing committees and the full membership of both houses. It is here, after the tumult

---

earnings to several hundred thousand dollars a year. "What we have is the expertise to show clients how the legislative or administrative decision-making process is likely to work in a given case," explained Walker. See "Superlobbyist," *Forbes*, September 15, 1973, p. 117.

45. Salamon, *op. cit.*, pp. 133–135.

and shouting and public debate have faded from the House and Senate and after the headlines have shifted to a new subject, that appropriations measures, tax bills and other substantive legislation can suffer remarkable mutation.[46]

A majority of both the House and Senate delegations to the conference committee, acting separately, must agree to the compromises. Since the committee chairmen appoint the conferees from their respective committees, Patman was in a strong position to influence the final outcome. Even though four of the five Senate conferees were sympathetic to the large banks, they could not overcome the 4–3 Patman majority on the House side of the joint committee. At the same time, the Patman forces were in a very poor bargaining position because the Senate bill was so extremely weak.

The first problem facing Patman and his colleagues was to get rid of a glaring loophole without compromising everything else they cared about. Nicknamed the Green Stamp Amendment because it had been proposed by a lobbyist from the holding company which controls S & H Green Stamps, the loophole permitted conglomerates controlling banks with less than $500 million in deposits to escape banking regulation. The Patman forces devised a successful strategy that appealed to the crassest of special-interest motives:

The Senate had fortuitously tacked on to its version of the holding company bill a noncontroversial provision for the coinage of 150 million commemorative Eisenhower dollars with a 40 percent silver content. Senator Wallace Bennett strongly favored this provision, since his home state, Utah, had a substantial silver industry. More important, the major contractor for the silver jacketing material used in the coins was a Massachusetts subsidiary of Englehard Industries, a corporation owned by Charles Englehard of Newark, New Jersey, who just hap-

46. Sherrill, *op. cit.*, p. 90.

pened to be a major contributor to the New Jersey Democratic party and to Senator Harrison Williams, the sponsor of the Green Stamp Amendment. Several of the House committee staff informed Englehard's Washington representative that the House conferees would reject the commemorative-medal provision unless Englehard demanded that Williams stop pressing his Green Stamp Amendment; in exchange Englehard would contribute to William's campaign for reelection. Apparently the deal worked, for on the first day of the conference, Williams agreed to drop his support for the amendment, and it died.[47]

Once the Green Stamp Amendment was out of the way, the key issue concerned what kind of nonbanking businesses could be owned by bank holding companies. The bill that emerged was stronger than the Senate version, but weaker that the 1956 restrictions. It was no longer necessary for the nonbanking business to be financial or fiduciary in nature. It was enough if the Federal Reserve Board decided that 1) the business was "so closely related to banking or managing or controlling banks as to be properly incident thereto," and 2) the benefits to the public were greater than any "adverse effects."[48] The compromise bill passed the house by 365–4. The Senate passed it by voice vote.

The history of the Bank Holding Amendments Act of 1970 is not very different from what might be found in any number of case studies of major congressional committees where business interests are at stake. However, even the results of this study might be interpreted as evidence for their view by many pluralists. They could emphasize that elected officials played a central role, that many different interests had an input and that no one interest got quite what it wanted.

The ruling-class interpretation of the legislative process in this case would be the one often heard on Capitol Hill—that the

47. *Ibid.*, p. 139.
48. *Ibid.*, p. 141.

banks never lose.[49] For if the final bill took one step forward in bringing the new one-bank holding companies under some kind of regulation, it took two steps backward in allowing all bank holding companies to own a wider range of businesses than had been permitted in the past. If the Federal Reserve Board now had to approve each acquisition, the fact remains that the board has since approved ownership of a wide range of businesses: "After all, when the First National City Corporation can offer its customers the opportunity to lease a Citibank-owned steamship fleet as part of its 'closely related' banking business, what is left in the nonbanking category?"[50] And certainly the growth of bank holding companies was not deterred. When the legislative effort began in early 1969, there were 684 bank holding companies controlling 40 percent of all bank deposits. By 1972, two years after the act was passed, there were 1,500 bank holding companies controlling 58 percent of total deposits.[51] In short, the tug and pull of the special-interest process, despite some minor victories for small-business forces, was dominated by the major banks.

THE LIMITS OF SPECIAL-INTEREST MECHANISMS

If a theorist is predisposed to a ruling-class view, the type of case study information presented in this chapter might seem on its face to be excellent evidence for the thesis that a ruling class dominates government in corporate America. This evidence shows how the corporate rich are able to realize their will on innumerable issues of concern to them. They are able to capture regula-

49. *Ibid.*, p. xxi.
50. *Ibid.*, p. 144.
51. *Ibid.*

tory agencies, advise executive departments and lobby the
Congress with a great deal of success. However, for those who
do not already believe there is a ruling class due to the very nature
of the capitalist system or on the basis of wealth and income statistics, this material is not sufficient evidence. It only demonstrates the power of specific interests, not the power of a class.

This argument is made most clearly and forcefully in Grant
McConnell's *Private Power and American Democracy*, which
marshals considerable evidence for big-business power within
government, but does not see the findings as supportive of a
ruling-class theory.[52] McConnell shows the ways in which various
interest groups have captured "pieces of government authority"
that are relevant to the interests of the groups.[53] He reviews the
twentieth-century history of congressional investigations into the
great influence of lobbyists and the capture of regulatory agencies
by those who are supposed to be regulated, noting that "the
record of exposure of this sort is one of almost tiresome repetition."[54] He provides the best analysis yet written of the advisory
committees that were later to be investigated by Senator Metcalf,
calling attention to their great influence through his study of
earlier government documents.

McConnell concludes from his detailed examination of interest-
group activity that "A large number of groups have achieved
substantial autonomy for themselves and the isolation of important
segments of government and public policy"; there has been a
"conquest of formal state power by private groups and associations."[55] McConnell draws a less sanguine conclusion from the
existence of interest groups than do most social scientists, putting
him at odds with the pluralistic majority:

52. (Knopf, 1966).
53. *Ibid.*, p. 7.
54. *Ibid.*, p. 21.
55. *Ibid.*, pp. 7 and 162.

The large extent of autonomy accorded to various fragments of government has gone far to isolate important matters of public policy from supposedly countervailing influences. Moreover, the picture of government as mediator among different interests is falsified to the extent that government itself is fragmented and the various fragments are beholden to particular interests.[56]

In addition, McConnell shows that some interests are more powerful than others. In discussing the politics of labor, for example, he makes it clear that organized labor has not had nearly the success of organized business groups within the governmental arena. Although the AF of L was successful in gaining a separate Labor Department in 1913, "the new Department's powers did not develop in the same manner as those of its counterparts elsewhere in government."[57] Nor has the labor movement been able to capture the regulatory agency important to it, the National Labor Relations Board. Unlike other regulatory agencies, which are dominated by business sectors, the NLRB has "a double constituency—management as well as labor."[58]

Despite his emphasis on business power and the relative weakness of labor, McConnell does not come to the conclusion that there is a ruling class in the United States. This is because the various business interests are not united and are not able to dominate the government as a whole. Only under the most exceptional of circumstances are they able to become even somewhat united, and most often they are not very interested in trying to influence broader policy issues like foreign policy, labor, fiscal policy and taxation:

56. *Ibid.*, p. 164.

57. *Ibid.*, p. 302. For some of the ways in which the Labor Department has been kept from becoming an outpost for the labor movement, see Nancy K. DiTomaso, "The Department of Labor: Class Politics and Public Bureaucracy," unpublished Ph.D. dissertation, Univ. of Wisconsin, 1977.

58. McConnell, *op. cit.*, pp. 306 and 318.

The first conclusion that emerges from the present analysis and survey is that a substantial part of government in the United States has come under the influence or control of narrowly based and largely autonomous elites. These elites do not "rule" in the sense of commanding the entire nation. Quite the contrary, they tend to pursue a policy of non-involvement in the large issues of statesmanship, save where such issues touch their own particular concerns.[59]

Because of their fragmentation and lack of clear intentions, the corporate elite have not been able to capture the whole of government. In McConnell's view, the units of government and politics which appeal to larger constituencies are not controlled by business groups: "It is not true that every unit of government and every bit of public authority is captive to some tight cohesive interest group with unfailingly cunning leadership."[60] The most important of these other units is the presidency:

The constituency of this majestic office is all the people. The prestige of its occupant is so great that when his power is husbanded and skillfully used he can make innovations of policy in the interest of those who are outside the pluralist scheme of rule.[61]

McConnell also sees the party system as a political mechanism with the potential to transcend the special interests. In particular, presidential elections force parties to rise above parochial and local interests. Finally, the Supreme Court usually functions as

59. *Ibid.*, p. 339. For the assertion that "this elite [the corporate elite] is incapable of exercising political domination save in exceptional circumstances and for very limited objectives and very limited times," see p. 254. For another expression of the claim that they only "occasionally become active in matters of large-scale policy such as taxation, foreign trade, labor and fiscal policy," see p. 292.

60. *Ibid.*, p. 351.

61. *Ibid.*

if its constituency were the whole nation.[62] The conclusion to McConnell's analysis appears as the last paragraph of his Introduction:

Fortunately, not all of American politics is based upon this array of small constituencies. The party system, the Presidency and the national government as a whole represent opposing tendencies. To a very great degree, policies serving the values of liberty and equality are the achievements of these institutions. Public values generally must depend upon the creation of a national constituency.[63]

The problems presented by McConnell's argument have been dealt with in one of two ways in the past by class-hegemony theorists. The first approach asserts that the sum total of the activities of the special interests *is* class rule. This argument emphasizes that what is *not* done and *not* debated defines ruling-class domination even if the class as a whole does not act consciously to realize its will and to subordinate other classes. Needless to say, this argument is not very impressive to social scientists of McConnell's persuasion, for it merely denies the implications of their analysis and asserts the opposite to be the case.

A second answer has been supplied by European Marxist Claus Offe. He accepts the empirical claims of the McConnell argument, but then goes on to say that it is the governmental apparatus itself which provides the overall plans and systemic integration that cannot be provided by narrow interest groups. Whereas McConnell believes that government in general is responsive to the public that elected it, Offe claims the government responds to the general needs of the corporate capitalist system. In this view, the government is a somewhat independent structure which is able to provide the necessary coordination of capitalist

62. *Ibid.*, pp. 351–352.
63. *Ibid.*, p. 8.

interests precisely because its relative autonomy allows it to transcend the demands of the special interests. This answer is not any more satisfactory than the first. It merely rejects the claim that the presidency and the parties reflect the public interest by asserting the "autonomy" of the state apparatus, an autonomy that is said to be maintained by "mystifying" the relationship between the state and the capitalist system.[64] It also ignores the absence of bureaucracies and agencies within the American government that are independent of special interests. Finally, as will be shown in the next chapter, the hypothetical answer provided by Offe flies in the face of the empirical reality of how class coordination actually is attained in the United States.

McConnell's objections to a ruling-class view are serious ones that call for a level of analysis that has not been forthcoming from proponents of that theory. To answer McConnell, it is necessary to show that the various special interests are in fact concerned about the larger issues, and that they are cohesive enough to formulate policies in regard to these issues. Moreover, it is essential to demonstrate how their general policies are transmitted to the presidency itself, for it is indeed the White House which initiates most of the innovations of policy within the national government.

There is recent evidence that the special interests are not as fragmented in dealing with Congress and executive bureaucracies as McConnell claimed from his vantage point in the mid-1960's. In particular, there is evidence that they cooperate in their lobbying efforts. Each year since 1950, it has been discovered, major business groups join with the American Farm Bureau Federation, the American Bar Association and the American Medical Associa-

---

64. Claus Offe, "Structural Problems of the Capitalist State," in Klaus von Beyme, ed., *German Political Studies* (Sage Publications, 1974). For similar views, see David A. Gold et al., "Recent Developments in Marxist Theories of the Capitalist State," *Monthly Review*, November, 1975.

tion for an annual Greenbrier Conference—named after the plush hotel in the resort town of White Sulphur Springs, West Virginia, where they meet—to map out their lobbying strategy for the coming year.[65] Moreover, studies of votes taken on a wide variety of legislation suggest that business, organized medicine, corporate law and the biggest farm organizations are generally united in their views, with labor unions, middle-level liberal organizations and minority-group organizations lined up on the other side. This division comes very close to the kind of class division that would be expected by class-hegemony theorists.[66]

However, even if it could be shown that the various business interest groups were completely coordinated on many special-interest issues and that any conflicts among them were on specific rather than general issues (as they usually are), this would not be a satisfactory answer to the kind of argument that McConnell presents. In fact, general policies are not developed and impressed upon government through any of the organizations or associations or mechanisms discussed in this chapter. Moreover, none of the books footnoted here recognizes this fact, which is why they do not begin to answer McConnell's objections despite their detailed cataloguing of bribes, subsidies, tax breaks and influence-peddling. They do not give their readers the slightest hint of how policy on the big issues—foreign policy, fiscal policy, population policy, welfare spending, the environment—is developed.

65. Donald R. Hall, *Cooperative Lobbying—The Power of Pressure* (Univ. of Arizona Press, 1969). Hall's book also describes several other methods of cooperative lobbying in addition to the Greenbrier Conference. Until it was published, the only mentions of the Greenbrier Conference were in two excellent books by journalists, Wesley McCune's *Who's Behind Our Farm Policy* (Praeger, 1956) and James Deakin's *The Lobbyists* (Public Affairs Press, 1966).

66. Edward Malecki, "Union Efforts to Influence Non-Labor Policies," unpublished M.A. thesis, Univ. of Illinois, 1963; Albert P. Melone, *Lawyers, Public Policy and Interest Group Politics* (Univ. Press of America, 1977).

In order to deal with the argument presented by McConnell—and by implication many other nonruling-class theorists—it is necessary to explore the policy-formation network that sustains the process by which proposals and programs on the larger issues are formulated. It is to this little-known and seldom-studied process that we will turn in the next chapter.

3
The
Policy-Formation
Process

The policy-formation process is the means by which the power elite formulates policy on larger issues. It is within the organizations of the policy-planning network that the various special interests join together to forge, however slowly and gropingly, the general policies that will benefit them as a whole. It is within the policy process that the various sectors of the business community transcend their interest-group consciousness and develop an overall class consciousness.

The staid and dignified policy-formation process is very different from the helter-skelter special-interest process. It appears to be as detached from day-to-day events as the special-interest process seems totally immersed in them. It appears as disinterested and fair-minded as the special-interest process seems self-seeking and biased. Whereas the special-interest process is usually staffed by lesser members of the power elite, the men and women of the policy-formation network are often from the "oldest" and wealthiest of families, the biggest and most powerful of corporations, and the most prestigious of law schools and university institutes. It is a world where "expertise" and a mild disdain for the special interests are the coin of the realm. Only the "national interest" is of concern. "Nonpartisan" and "objective" are the passwords.

The policy-formation process begins in corporate board rooms and executive suites. It ends in the innermost private offices of the government in Washington, where reporters and sociologists never tread. In between the beginning and the end there are a handful of huge foundations that provide the experts with money for research, as well as blue-ribbon presidential commissions which legitimate the policies to the general public and present them formally to the President. Research institutes and think tanks also are to be found in the inner circles of the network, and influential newspapers and magazines are important in bringing the views of the policy groups to the attention of government personnel. However, the central units in the policy network are such official-sounding organizations as the Council on Foreign Relations, the Committee for Economic Development, the Business Council and the American Assembly, which are best categorized as the policy-planning and consensus-seeking organizations of the power elite. They are also the training grounds in which new leaders for government service are informally selected. (An overview of the entire policy network appears in the diagram on the next page.)

The policy-discussion organizations bring together, in groups large and small, members of the power elite from all over the country to discuss general problems like overseas aid, tariffs, the use of nuclear weapons, tax problems, the population problem, labor relations and the targeting of national goals. They provide an off-the-record, informal setting in which differences on various issues can be thrashed out and the opinions of various experts can be heard. In addition to their numerous small-group discussions, these organizations encourage general dialogue within the power elite by means of luncheon and dinner speeches, special

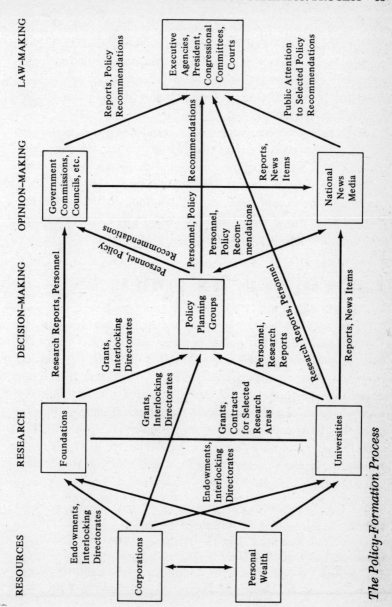

The Policy-Formation Process

written reports and position statements in journals and books. It was in these groups that the basis for capital-labor détente was worked out at the turn of the century, that the plans for Social Security were created, that the ideas behind the Marshall Plan were developed, and that the foreign policy of the Carter administration was formulated.

Since the policy-planning groups are at the center of things, they provide a good starting point for understanding the policy network as a whole. By discussing several of the major policy groups in a general way, it will be possible to show how they connect to the corporations and foundations on the one hand, and the government on the other, as well as to give a more concrete idea of how they function.

THE COUNCIL ON FOREIGN RELATIONS

The best known of the policy organizations is the Council on Foreign Relations. Founded in 1920–21 by East Coast bankers, lawyers and academicians who were fully cognizant of the enlarged role the United States would play in world affairs in the wake of World War I, the council's importance in shaping foreign policy has been noted by numerous journalists.[1] However, it has been the object of only two academic studies during its history, an impressive commentary in itself on how little social scientists know about policy-making in the United States.[2]

1. E.g., Joseph Kraft, "School for Statesmen," *Harper's* magazine, July, 1958; J. Anthony Lukas, "The Council on Foreign Relations—Is It a Club? Seminar? Presidium? 'Invisible Government'?" the *New York Times Magazine*, November 21, 1971.

2. G. William Domhoff, *The Higher Circles* (Random House, 1970), chapter 5; Laurence H. Shoup and William Minter, *Imperial Brain Trust* (Monthly Review Press, 1977).

There are about 1,500 members in the Council, half from the New York area, half from the rest of the country. The members are primarily financiers, executives and lawyers, with a strong minority of journalists and academic experts. The biggest banks and corporations are the most heavily represented organizations.[3] The council receives its general funding from wealthy individuals, corporations and subscriptions to its influential periodical, *Foreign Affairs*. For special projects, however, it relies upon major foundations for support. Especially important sources are the Ford, Rockefeller and Carnegie foundations, which have numerous director and executive interlocks with the council leadership.

The council operates an active program of luncheon and dinner speeches at its New York clubhouse, featuring major U.S. government officials and national leaders from all over the world. It also encourages dialogue and disseminates information through books, pamphlets and articles in *Foreign Affairs*. However, the most important aspect of the CFR program is its discussion groups and policy groups. These small gatherings of about twenty-five bring together business executives, government officials, scholars and military officers for detailed discussions of specific topics in the area of foreign affairs. Discussion groups are charged with exploring problems in a general way, trying to define issues and alternatives. Such groups often lead to a study group as the next stage.

Study groups revolve around the work of a council research fellow (financed by Ford, Rockefeller and Carnegie foundations) or a staff member. This group leader and other experts present monthly papers which are discussed and criticized by the rest of the group. The goal of such study groups is a detailed statement of the problem by the scholar leading the discussions.

In 1957–58, for example, the council published six books which grew out of study groups. The most famous of these, *Nuclear*

3. Shoup and Minter, *op. cit.*, chapter 3.

Weapons and Foreign Policy, was written by Harvard professor
Henry Kissinger, who had been asked by CFR leaders to head
the study group. The book received a very careful reading in
the Kennedy administration.[4] In addition to several bankers and
corporate executives, the Kissinger study group included two
former appointees in the upper echelons of the Defense Department, two former chairpersons of the Atomic Energy Commission
and representatives from just below the top level at the State
Department, the CIA and all three armed forces.

Study groups at the Council on Foreign Relations have been
at the heart of many foreign policy initiatives. The post–World
War II planning which led to the formation of the International
Monetary Fund, World Bank and United Nations was a council
project, as will be demonstrated in detail later in the chapter. A
series of study groups in the 1940's and 1950's helped to establish
the consensus wisdom that it was necessary to "defend" Vietnam
at any cost.[5] A $1-million grant from the Ford and Rockefeller
foundations in the early 1960's led to study groups which recon-
sidered U.S. policy toward China, finally concluding that the
policy must be changed to one of recognition and eventual trade
relations.[6]

Many council members are directly involved in the making
of foreign policy in Washington. "Over a third of the Council's
1500 members have been called on by the government during
the last 20 years to undertake official responsibilities," reports a
council publication.[7] "Whenever we needed a man," explained one
of the lawyers who ran the Department of War in World War II,
"we thumbed through a roll of Council members and put through

4. Kraft, *op. cit.*, p. 66.
5. Shoup and Minter, *op. cit.*, chapter 6.
6. *Ibid.*, pp. 207–212.
7. "Programs and Purposes: Studies on Foreign Policy 1970–1971" (Council on Foreign Relations, 1971).

a call to New York."[8] Twelve of the fourteen "wise men" who were President Lyndon B. Johnson's secret Senior Advisory Group on Vietnam were members of the council.[9] And all but one or two of the major appointments to the State Department by President Jimmy Carter in 1977 were members of the council.

THE COMMITTEE FOR ECONOMIC DEVELOPMENT

The Committee for Economic Development (CED) was founded in the early 1940's to help plan for the postwar world. The corporate leaders who were the driving force in CED had two major concerns at that time: 1) there might be another major depression after the war; 2) if businesspeople did not present plans for the postwar era, other sectors of society might present plans that were not acceptable to businesspeople.[10] The CED expressly was trying to avoid any identification with special-interest pleading:

The Committee would avoid "promoting the special interests of business itself as such" and would likewise refrain from speaking for any other special interests. . . . The CED was to be a businessman's organization that would speak in the national interest.[11]

The CED consisted of 200 corporate leaders in its early years. Later it was to include a handful of university presidents among its members. In addition, leading economists have served as re-

8. Kraft, *op. cit.*, p. 67.

9. Shoup and Minter, *op. cit.*, p. 242.

10. David Eakins, "The Development of Corporate Liberal Policy Research in the United States, 1885–1965," unpublished Ph.D. dissertation, Univ. of Wisconsin, 1966, p. 340.

11. *Ibid.*, p. 346.

search advisors to the CED; many have gone on to serve in advisory roles in both Republican and Democratic administrations, and particularly on the Council of Economic Advisers. Although there is an overlap in membership with the Council on Foreign Relations, the committee has a different mix of members. Unlike the council, it has few bankers, and no corporate lawyers, journalists and academic experts. This gives the organization a more conventional and less liberal cast.

Like the council, the CED works through study groups which are aided by academic experts. The study groups have considered every conceivable general issue from farm policy to government reorganization to the social responsibility of corporations, but the greater emphasis is on economic issues of both a domestic and international nature. The most ambitious of committee projects usually have been financed by the Ford Foundation.

Unlike the larger CFR, which would find it cumbersome to reach an "official" position on any given issue, the results of committee study groups are released as official policy statements of the organization. The statements are published in pamphlet form and disseminated widely in business, government and media circles. There is reason to believe that many of these reports have had considerable influence, for there is a striking similarity between CED statements and policies that were enacted shortly thereafter.[12]

The fact that committee trustees are tapped for government service also lends credence to the idea that the organization has a policy impact. Of the 150 men who were CED trustees between 1942 and 1957, 38 served in government posts in both Republican and Democratic administrations.[13] In 1971 five committee trustees

12. *Ibid.*, chapters 7 and 8; Karl Schriftgiesser, *Business and Public Policy* (Prentice-Hall, 1967).

13. Karl Schriftgiesser, *Business Comes of Age* (Harper & Row, 1960), p. 162.

were in the Nixon administration. In the Carter administration, CED trustees served as Secretary of the Treasury and Secretary of the Navy, and the former chairperson of the CED Research Advisory Board was the head of the Council of Economic Advisers.

THE CONFERENCE BOARD

The Conference Board, founded in 1916 as the National Industrial Conference Board, is the oldest of the existing policy-discussion groups. It was originally a more narrowly focused organization with a primary interest within the business community itself. During the 1930's and 1940's it drifted to an extreme right-wing stance under the influence of its executive director, who often denounced other policy groups for their alleged desertion of the free-enterprise system.[14] Only with the retirement of this director in 1948 did the board move back into the mainstream and begin to assume its current role as a major voice of big business. Further change in the 1960's was symbolized by the shortening of its name to Conference Board and the election of a CED trustee as its president. By 1977, when its president was selected by President Carter to chair the Federal Reserve Board, it was one of the most central and important of the policy groups.

The Conference Board has been innovative in developing international linkages. In 1961, in conjunction with the Stanford Research Institute, the board sponsored a week-long International Industrial Conference in San Francisco. This international gathering brought together 500 leaders in industry and finance from 60 countries to hear research reports and discuss common problems. The International Industrial Conference has met every four

14. Eakins, *op. cit.*, chapter 5.

years since that time. Along with the "sister" committees which the CED has encouraged in numerous nations, the International Industrial Conference is one of the major institutions in the international policy discussion network that has been growing slowly since the 1950's.

THE BUSINESS COUNCIL

Grant McConnell had only one hesitation in suggesting that the politics of business were conducted in narrow interest groups. That was the existence of the Business Council. Calling it "one of the more remarkable groups ever associated with the government," McConnell based his account on the small amount of information on its advisory functions that investigators had been able to obtain from the tight-lipped Department of Commerce up until the mid 1960's.[15]

McConnell noted that in the 1940's and 1950's the Council included a cross-section of the major business leaders in the nation. It held six meetings a year, some in Washington, some in resort settings like Sea Island, Georgia and Hot Springs, Virginia. Major government officials were in attendance at the meetings, which were strictly confidential. The council also prepared reports on a wide variety of general issues to give to government leaders. The expenses for meetings and reports were paid by private contributions.

The Business Council, which was created in 1933 as an adjunct to the Department of Commerce, made a unilateral withdrawal from its quasi-governmental status in 1962 because of a small flap with the Kennedy administration. North Carolina businessman Luther H. Hodges, serving as Kennedy's Secretary of Com-

15. Grant McConnell, *Private Power and American Democracy* (Knopf, 1966), p. 276.

merce, asked the council to include more small-business representatives and to allow reporters to cover its meetings. He was responding in part to congressional and journalistic criticisms of the council's exclusive relationship with government, and in part to the fact that its chairperson at the time, Ralph Cordiner of General Electric, was in the limelight because of a gigantic price-fixing scandal in the electrical equipment industry. Rather than totally accept Hodges' suggestions, the Business Advisory Council, as it was then called, quietly told the government that it was changing its name to the Business Council and becoming an independent organization which would offer its advice to all agencies of the government.

Despite the fact that the Business Council was no longer an official advisory group to the Department of Commerce, it continued the prominent role it had developed during the Eisenhower administration, supplying businesspeople for government positions and meeting regularly in Hot Springs with government officials. It was especially close to the Johnson administration.[16]

McConnell considers the possibility that the Business Council might be "a directorate of big business effectually controlling the economic policy of the nation," but dismisses the idea on the following grounds:

Certainly, if a search were to be made for a top executive committee of corporate business, no more likely body could be found than the Business Council. Nevertheless, such an interpretation would probably be mistaken. The Council included a number of disparate elements. Not only were some representatives of small business actually members, but some of the representatives of big business had interests in conflict with each other. Moreover, the recommendations of the Council have not always been put into effect.[17]

16. Hobart Rowan, *The Free Enterprisers* (G. P. Putnam's Sons, 1964), p. 77.

17. McConnell, *op. cit.*, p. 279.

In the end, McConnell sees the Business Council as a more ideological group, and also as a social group which confers prestige on its members. It is thus less important to its big-business members than industry advisory committees: ". . . membership on the National Petroleum Council has probably been more important than membership on the Business Advisory Council to Mr. Eugene Holman, Chairman of the Board of Standard Oil of New Jersey [Exxon]; much the same thing could probably be said of other figures of high stature in business."[18]

McConnell's perceptions of the Business Council are symptomatic, for they show the failure to distinguish between narrow interest-group advisory committees and general policy groups. It is in this inclusion of both types of organizations in a single analytical category that the policy process is lost from view. In singling out the Business Council for further discussion, McConnell rightfully put his finger on an organization that has a significant place in the policy-planning process, but did not explore adequately its unique role.

The council does not conduct as many study groups or hold as many meetings as do most policy-discussion organizations. Indeed, it was because the Business Council had only limited research capabilities that the Committee for Economic Development was formed. Nonetheless, the Business Council is centrally situated in the policy-planning network. It is a collecting and consensus-seeking point for much of the work of the other organizations. Moreover, it is one of the few organizations that has regular and formal meetings with government officials. It is, then, a major connection between big business and government. In a way, its centrality among the policy groups makes it the unofficial board of directors within the power elite.

Many Washington observers have made this claim about the centrality of the Business Council from impressionistic informa-

18. *Ibid.*

tion, but the point also can be made more systematically. In one study, membership overlaps among thirty-one social clubs and policy groups were analyzed mathematically to determine the centrality score for each organization. The Business Council emerged as the most central organization, rivaled only by the Committee for Economic Development.[19]

In a second study based on the overlapping members in thirty-six clubs and policy groups, another mathematical technique was used to determine the pattern of relationships among the groups. This study uncovered two cliques that were primarily rooted in organizations on the East and West Coasts, respectively, and a third clique whose members were linked to both the East and West Coast cliques. The Business Council was a member of this integrating clique, along with the Committee for Economic Development, the Conference Board and several social clubs.[20]

Because it cultivates what a congressional committee called "an aura of secrecy," there is very little systematic evidence on the functioning of the Council. However, one of my former research assistants undertook a careful observational study for me of its May 1972 meeting. The four-day gathering was held in the lavish Homestead Hotel in Hot Springs, Virginia, a town of less

19. G. William Domhoff, "Social Clubs, Policy-Planning Groups and Corporations: A Network Study of Ruling-Class Cohesiveness," *The Insurgent Sociologist,* Spring, 1975.

20. Philip Bonacich and G. William Domhoff, "Overlapping Memberships Among Clubs and Policy Groups of the American Ruling Class," paper presented at the annual meeting of the American Sociological Association, Chicago, 1977. Using an entirely different approach based on interviews with businesspeople and the leaders of business groups, sociologist Floyd Hunter arrived at the same result in 1959—the Conference Board, the Committee for Economic Development and the Business Council are at the heart of the national power structure. See Floyd Hunter, *Top Leadership U.S.A.* (Univ. of North Carolina Press, 1959), p. 33.

than 2,500 people, 50 miles from Washington. Council members heard speeches by government officials, conducted panels on problems of general concern, received reports from hired staff and talked informally with each other and the government officials in attendance.

The meetings were held in a relaxed and friendly atmosphere that reinforced the feeling of camaraderie between the business and government participants. Discussion sessions were alternated with social events, including golf tournaments, tennis matches and banquet-style dinners for members, guests and wives. The guest list included the chairman of the Federal Reserve System, the Secretary of the Army, the Director of the CIA, the Secretary of State, the Secretary of Commerce, the Chairman of the Council of Economic Advisers and a Special Assistant to the President.[21]

Very little is known about the role the council has played in urging the government to adopt any specific policies, mainly because it will not make its files available for research. However, a careful historical study of the council's history is highly persuasive in arguing that it had little impact on government policy during its early years, when it was little more than an adjunct to the Department of Commerce.[22] Its only real domestic success throughout the New Deal was its supportive involvement in the Social Security Act.[23] It was not until the Eisenhower adminis-

21. See Craig Kubey, "Notes on a Meeting of the Business Council," *The Insurgent Sociologist*, Spring, 1973, for a summary account of this study.

22. Kim McQuaid, "The Business Advisory Council of the Department of Commerce, 1933–1961: A Study of Corporate/Government Relations," Paul U. Selding, ed., *Research in Economic History*, Volume 1 (JAI Press, 1976).

23. Domhoff, *The Higher Circles, op. cit.*, pp. 210–215. The council also played a very central role in creating and managing the National Labor Board and labor advisory boards in specific industries in the years 1933–35. However, these efforts in "self-regulation" did not work out and were

tration that it began to assume its present role. Since that time it has been a major contact point between the corporate community and the executive branch, providing government officials with direct presentations of the policy perspectives developed in the rest of the network, and serving as a stepping stone to government service for its members.[24]

SATELLITES AND THINK TANKS

The Council on Foreign Relations, Committee for Economic Development, Conference Board and Business Council are the Big Four of the policy network, but they do not function in isolation. They are surrounded by a variety of satellites and think tanks which operate in specialized areas or provide research information and expert advisors for the Big Four.

The National Planning Association, for example, is a small policy-discussion group which took its present form in 1942 as part of the concern with postwar planning. It has a more liberal outlook than the CED, but has been very close to it. In the mid-1950's the two organizations considered a merger, but decided against it because the NPA has a distinctive role to play in that both its leadership and study groups include representatives from labor and agriculture: "NPA did not want to lose the frankness and open interchange it achieved through labor participation, and CED felt it had acquired a reputation for objectivity and

superseded by the National Labor Relations Act of 1935, an act that was opposed by most members of the council. I am grateful to Professor Kim McQuaid for providing me with access to his original research on this topic through personal communications.

24. Frank V. Fowlkes, "Business Council Shuns Lobbying but Influences Federal Policy," *National Journal*, November 20, 1971, presents interview evidence of council influence.

did not wish to dilute this good will toward an avowedly business organization by bringing in other groups."[25]

Similarly, a policy-discussion group started in the early 1950's, the American Assembly, has many links to the CED, and once considered merger with it. Once again, the merger idea was dropped because the American Assembly has a unique function. Its twice-a-year meetings on a variety of general issues include labor and farm leaders as well as businesspeople and academics. Moreover, the assembly has a greater outreach program to upper-middle-income groups and students through books, pamphlets and a series of regional and local "Little Assemblies" based on the same topics discussed at the semi-annual national meetings in New York.[26]

The deepest and most critical thinking within the policy network does not take place in the policy-discussion groups, as many academicians who have taken part in them are quick to point out. While this claim may be in part self-serving by professors who like to assume they are smarter than businesspeople and bankers, there is no question but that many new initiatives are created in various think tanks before they are brought to the discussion groups for modification and assimilation by the corporate leaders. There are dozens of these think tanks, some highly specialized to one or two topics.[27] Among the most important are the RAND Corporation, the Stanford Research Institute, the Urban Institute, the National Bureau of Economic Research, Resources for the Future and the Center for International Studies at MIT. The institutes and centers connected to universities receive much of their funding from foundations, while the large and less special-

25. Eakins, *op. cit.*, p. 479.

26. *Ibid.*, pp. 465–471.

27. See Paul Dickson, *Think Tanks* (Atheneum, 1971), for a description of the major think tanks.

ized independent think tanks are more likely to undertake contract research for businesses or government agencies.

Some organizations are hybrids that incorporate both think-tank and policy-discussion functions. They do not fit neatly into one category or the other. Such is the case with one of the most important institutions in the policy network, The Brookings Institution. This large organization is directed by big business-people, but it is not a membership organization. It conducts study groups for businesspeople and government officials, but it is even more important as a kind of postgraduate school for expert advisors. Employing a very large number of social scientists, it functions as a source of new ideas and sophisticated consultants for policy groups and government leaders. In particular, its economists have served both Republican and Democratic administrations since its founding in 1927. It has been especially close to the CED since the 1950's, but it also has strong ties to the Council on Foreign Relations and the American Assembly.[28]

Several hybrids function in specialized areas. The Population Council was established in 1952 to fund research and develop policy on population control. Relying on large personal donations from John D. Rockefeller III and several foundations, it helped to create population research institutes at major universities, held conferences and publicized its findings. Case studies reveal that it has done very well indeed in getting its message across.[29] Resources for the Future was founded about the same time as the Population Council, with funds from the Ford Foundation. It has

28. Eakins, *op. cit.*; Bonacich and Domhoff, *op. cit.*

29. William Barclay, Joseph Enright and Reid T. Reynolds, "Population Control in the Third World," *NACLA Newsletter*, December, 1970; Steve Weissman, "Why the Population Bomb Is a Rockefeller Baby," *Ramparts*, May, 1970; Phyllis T. Piotrow, *World Population Crisis: The United States Response* (Praeger, 1973).

become one of the power elite's major sources of information and policy on environmental issues, although it has to share this role with the Conservation Foundation, the American Conservation Association and three or four other closely related organizations.[30] In the issue-area of education, and in particular higher education, the Carnegie Corporation has played a central role through a series of special commissions.[31] There are also corporate-financed groups in the areas of farm policy, municipal government and even the arts, for the arts are considered by some executives to be important in maintaining the morale of inner-city residents.[32]

All of these more specialized groups are linked by funding and common directors to the biggest foundations, major policy-discussion groups and largest banks and corporations. Council on Foreign Relations members and trustees tend to dominate in the population establishment, and CED trustees are more evident in farm groups, but these differences are nuances within a general picture of cohesion. Sometimes the specialized groups lend their services to the discussion groups of the larger organizations. They often are listed as advisors on specialized CED policy statements.

30. Katherine Barkley and Steve Weissman, "The Eco-Establishment," *Ramparts*, May, 1970; Peter Collier and David Horowitz, *The Rockefellers: An American Dynasty* (Holt, 1976), pp. 305–306, 384–385, and 401.

31. Merle Curti and Roderick Nash, *Philanthropy in the Shaping of American Higher Education* (Rutgers Univ. Press, 1965); David N. Smith, *Who Rules the Universities?* (Monthly Review Press, 1974); and Frank Darknell, "The Carnegie Council for Policy Studies in Higher Education: A New Policy Group for the Ruling Class," *The Insurgent Sociologist*, Spring, 1975.

32. Wesley McCune, *Who's Behind Our Farm Policy* (Praeger, 1956); Frank M. Stewart, *A Half Century of Municipal Reform* (Univ. of California Press, 1950); Arnold Gingrich, *Business and the Arts* (Paul S. Eriksson, 1969).

THE BUSINESS ROUNDTABLE

The most recent and atypical organization to join the policy network is the Business Roundtable, founded in early 1973 by the chairpersons of several dozen of the largest corporations in the nation. The Business Roundtable is in many ways the lobbying counterpart of the Business Council, with which it has numerous common members. In 1976, 33 of the 45 leaders of the Business Roundtable also were members of the Business Council. While the Business Council prefers to remain in the background and focus on the Executive branch, the Business Roundtable is unique among general policy groups in that it has an activist profile and personally lobbies members of Congress as readily as it meets privately with the President and cabinet leaders. In 1976 *Business Week* called it "business' most powerful lobby in Washington."[33]

The Roundtable was created through the merger of three ad hoc business committees—the Construction Users Anti-Inflation Roundtable, which was originally organized to fight inflation in the construction industry; the Labor Law Study Committee, which worked for changes in labor laws; and the March Group, which was created to tell "business' story" via the mass media. The new group was formed because it was felt that corporate executives were relying too heavily on specific trade associations to do their lobbying. It was hoped that direct lobbying contact by the chief executives with legislators would have even more impact.[34]

The 150 member companies pay from $10,000 to $35,000 per

33. "Business' Most Powerful Lobby in Washington," *Business Week*, December 20, 1976, p. 63.

34. "Business Roundtable: Big Corporation Bastion," *Congressional Quarterly*, November 23, 1974; Peter Slavin, "The Business Roundtable: New Lobbying Arm of Big Business," *Business and Society Review*, Winter, 1975/1976.

year in dues, depending on their size. This provided a budget of $2.4 million in 1976. Membership in the organization is open, but it is not solicited. Decisions on where the Roundtable will direct its money and prestige are ultimately determined by a forty-person policy committee which meets every two months to discuss current public issues, create task forces to study selected issues and review position papers prepared by task forces. In developing its positions and strategies, the policy committee relies on task forces. Each is headed by the chief executive of a major company. Task forces avoid problems within a given industry. They concentrate on issues "that have a broad impact on business."[35]

With a staff of only nine people, including clerical help, the Roundtable does not have much capability for developing its own information. However, this presents no problem because task force members "often draw on the research capabilities of their own companies or the companies of other task force members."[36] In addition, the Business Roundtable, like the Business Council, is the beneficiary of the work of other organizations in the policy network, for most of the members of the policy committee are in one or more of these organizations.

So far the Roundtable has played a defensive role in Washington, stopping legislation rather than passing its own. It helped kill the proposed Consumer Protection Agency during the Ford administration, and then did the same during the Carter administration, even while working very closely with Carter on other issues.[37] The Roundtable also is credited with watering down federal antitrust legislation, including the deletion of an amendment which would have given the attorneys general of all fifty

35. *Business Week, op. cit.*, p. 63.
36. *Ibid.*
37. "Carter's Campaign to Placate Business," *Business Week*, November 29, 1976, p. 23.

states the authority to sue antitrust violators on behalf of the citizens of their states and collect money damages.[38] However, it failed in 1974 in its attempt to make it illegal for striking workers to collect food stamps.

It is too soon to tell if the Business Roundtable will play a permanent role within the policy network. The fact that it focuses on Congress and fights against legislation disliked by big business does give it a somewhat special niche within the larger network. On the other hand, organizations that lobby and become embroiled in conflict often outlive their usefulness after a few years. They get a bad name, and new organizations have to be created. Whatever the long-run fate of the Business Roundtable, it is useful to be reminded that new organizations are possible within a network that has been stable for many years.

ULTRACONSERVATIVE POLICY GROUPS

The policy network is not totally homogeneous. There are differences of opinion within it. Most of these conflicts are worked out within the privacy of the discussion groups. However, this is not always the case. Furthermore, there is an ultraconservative clique within the policy network that has consistent and long-standing disagreements with the organizations discussed so far. While the differences between the two factions seem to have decreased since the early 1960's, some of the more hysterical leaders among the ultraconservatives seem to believe that many moderate conservatives at the Council on Foreign Relations and the Committee for Economic Development are Communist-influenced "collectivists" who are destroying the economic sys-

38. Eileen Shanahan, "Antitrust Bill Stopped by a Business Lobby," the *New York Times*, November 16, 1975, p. 1.

tem. They have held this belief about moderate conservatives since the Progressive Era, despite considerable evidence to the contrary.

It is these ultraconservative organizations—the most prominent of which are the National Association of Manufacturers, the Chamber of Commerce of the United States, the American Enterprise Institute and the American Security Council—that are identified with "big business" in the eyes of most social scientists and the general public. The fact that they are generally naysayers and often lose on highly visible issues is one of the major reasons for the belief that the ruling class is not as powerful as class-hegemony theorists have portrayed it. What is not understood is that those setbacks are usually at the hands of their more moderate and soft-spoken brethren within the policy network and the corporate community.

The moderate conservatives and ultraconservatives have differed on foreign policy and welfare legislation, and in their attitudes toward organized labor. The moderates tend to be internationalist in foreign policy; the ultraconservatives tend to be isolationist. The moderates have created and supported many welfare-state measures; the ultraconservatives have opposed such measures. However, differences in these two areas have decreased somewhat in the last decade. The ultraconservatives have moderated their views on foreign policy; the moderates have hardened some of their views on welfare legislation.

The most persistent difference between the two camps has been on the issue of organized labor. Throughout the twentieth century, the moderates have understood that trade unions can be a stabilizing force which serves as a bulwark against socialism. They have been willing to bargain with unions when sectors of the working class have been militant enough to force the issue. For the ultraconservatives, unions are communism itself, or at least the forerunners of communism, and must be destroyed at any cost. The difference between the two approaches manifested itself at the turn of the century when the moderates invited labor leaders to join with them in a discussion group called the National Civic Federation. While the federation was slowly working out the ideological and political bargain with organized labor which provided part of the basis for the legal recognition of unions in the 1930's, ultraconservatives within the National Association of Manufacturers were obtaining court injunctions against the labor leaders with whom the federation was working.[39]

In more recent times, the Committee for Economic Development and the National Association of Manufacturers had a misunderstanding over right-to-work laws that reveals the continuing differences between the two approaches. In 1959 the CED asked several academic experts on labor-management relations to compose an independent report on appropriate labor policies for the 1960's. Although the report was not a committee policy statement, it incurred the wrath of the NAM when it appeared in 1962 because it was not highly critical of unions. It even suggested that antiunion right-to-work laws should be abolished. Several financial contributors to CED went so far as to withdraw their support over the incident. One ultraconservative corporate leader charged that the committee was being run by its staff—and that this subversive staff was using the money and prestige provided to it to injure "the interests of the very ones supplying the money for the effort—as well as progressively impairing the whole free-market, private property, limited government arrangement under which we have been able to have and enjoy freedom."[40] The leader to the staff in question was George P. Shultz, a professor of Industrial Relations in the graduate school of business at the University of Chicago. Shultz later served in the Nixon adminis-

39. James Weinstein, *The Corporate Ideal in the Liberal State* (Beacon Press, 1968), chapters 1–3 and 7.

40. William F. Rickenbacker, "CED: Tycoon Trap?" *National Review*, February 26, 1963, p. 156.

tration as Secretary of Treasury, then went on to be a vice president of Bechtel Corporation, one of the largest construction companies in the world.

The CED, whose own trustees were in considerable disagreement over the contents of the report, admitted that it had lived dangerously in order to obtain an independent view. It then appointed a study group of its own members to prepare an official policy statement on labor unions. Serving on this Labor Policy Subcommittee, among several, were the chairpersons of U.S. Steel, American Can, Montgomery Ward and Scott Paper. The report, published in 1964, was endorsed by the Research and Policy Committee as a whole, a group including chief executives from Bank of America, Exxon, Merck & Co., AT&T, Ford Motor Co. and Federated Department Stores. The new statement endorsed right-to-work laws and blamed unions for contributing to inflation. As committee historian Karl Schriftgiesser frankly stated, "In tone or substance, *Union Power and Union Functions* was not one of CED's happiest productions."[41]

While this incident revealed that the disagreements between CED and NAM on labor policy were relatively minor, there is a difference. Most leaders within the committee would allow unions to exist, although they would like them to be in an even weaker position than they are now. The association, on the other hand, would like to smash them. The difference also can be seen in the fact that the ultraconservatives would no more risk allowing professors to write an independent report for them on this delicate topic than they would consider having the Communist Party write one. The distinction is a subtle one, not always given to divergent policies, but it has manifested itself in a more reasonable response by the moderates in times of extreme crisis and labor militancy.

The similarity between conservatives and ultraconservatives

41. Schriftgiesser, *op. cit.*, p. 166.

on labor issues when unions are on the defensive was demonstrated in the suggestions offered by various policy groups in the year or two before the antiunion Taft-Hartley Act of 1948 was passed. Although major credit for the most drastic provisions of the act went to lawyers and economists working for the NAM and The Brookings Institution, an analysis of the amendments urged by moderate groups revealed that they had advocated many of the changes that were enacted.[42] Schriftgiesser called the CED position "mild" when "compared with demands from other organizations," but notes that many of the changes were similar to CED suggestions or in harmony with its overall views.[43]

There are some leadership interlocks among the CED, NAM and the chamber. Then too, many companies pay dues to all three. Generally speaking, however, the association and the chamber are closer to the smaller of the big corporations. A study from the 1960's showed that the businesspeople who were most isolationist, antiwelfare and antilabor were more likely to be in NAM and to be associated with smaller and more regional corporations. Those who were more moderate were more likely to be in CED and to manage larger companies.[44] More recently, our study of the corporate interlocks of CED and NAM leaders revealed the same large/small dichotomy. For example, NAM's directors for 1972 had only 9 connections to the top 25 banks, whereas CED had 63. Similarly, NAM had but 10 connections to the 25 largest industrials, while CED had 48. The findings were similar for insurance, transports, utilities and retails.

However, the small-business nature of NAM can be pushed too far. A study of NAM directors throughout this century

42. Eakins, *op. cit.*, pp. 414–418.

43. Schriftgiesser, *op. cit.*, pp. 161–162.

44. Charles E. Woodhouse and David S. McLellan, "American Business Leaders and Foreign Policy: A Study in Perspectives," *The American Journal of Economics and Sociology*, July, 1966.

showed that it was at its most reactionary in the 1930's shortly after it was taken over by big businesspeople connected with the Du Pont interests.[45] Then too, our study of NAM leadership showed that vice presidents and public relations people from the very largest corporations now join with the chief executives of smaller businesses in managing the affairs of the association.

The secondary nature of NAM in recent years can be seen in the fact that it almost suffered a merger with the chamber in 1976. Although the proposed merger was advertised as one between equals, it was clear to most observers that NAM was the junior partner, suffering from declining membership and revenues.[46] The new organization, to be called the Association of Commerce and Industry, was to be housed in the chamber's large building across from the White House; NAM would have added only $8 million to the chamber's healthy income of $24.1 million a year.

In addition to the merger, there was talk of asking the Business Roundtable to serve as an advisory policy council for the new organization. This possibility was not without its critics. "When they do that," said one of them, "they will make the Roundtable the board of directors of the ACI."[47] The leader of the new organization was to be R. Heath Larry, vice chairperson of U.S. Steel and a trustee of the CED. With a U.S. Steel executive slated to take over as chair, and the Business Roundtable looming as a board of directors, it is not surprising that executives from smaller corporations were apprehensive. It would signal domination by the biggest of the big over the two broad-gauge business groups where they still had a voice:

45. Philip H. Burch, Jr., "The NAM as an Interest Group," *Politics and Society*, Fall, 1973.
46. "Business Lobbyists Blend Their Voices," *Business Week*, June 21, 1976, p. 31.
47. *Ibid.*

The biggest question regarding the future of the ACI revolves around the role large corporations will play in setting its policies. Already, some small business advocates within both groups fear these corporations will dominate. "Clearly, this merger was decided by the heads of the major corporations," says one source close to the negotiations.[48]

When the merger was announced, it had been approved by the executive committees of both organizations. It still had to be cleared by the boards of directors, but the presidents of the two organizations said there was little doubt the merger would be completed.[49] To everyone's surprise, the NAM directors rejected the plan, suggesting instead a joint policy council to coordinate on "key issues."[50] This rejection symbolizes the continuing tension between big and small corporations on some policy issues. It suggests that the time is not yet for the policy network to become a completely harmonious whole.

PRESIDENTIAL COMMISSIONS

As is evident from the discussion of specific policy groups, members and organizations of the policy-formation network have no trouble in getting their views heard by government. However, there is one connection to government that is an institution in itself. This is the practice of appointing a presidential commission.

Presidential commissions are specially appointed temporary committees made up primarily, if not totally, of private citizens. They gather information, deliberate and report to the President on the topic assigned to them. Their use is not without precedent

48. *Ibid.*

49. "Chamber, NAM Agree to Merge," San Francisco *Chronicle*, June 8, 1976, p. 49.

50. "NAM Rejects a Merger," *Business Week*, November 1, 1976, p. 32.

in the nineteenth century, but they really came into their own in the turn-of-the-century administration of Theodore Roosevelt. Since that time there has been a fairly steady growth in their employment by chief executives, especially since World War II.

Commissions can serve several functions. Some are meant to cool out public opinion on an issue that has caused a sense of urgency in the general public—such was the role of various commissions which investigated ghetto uprisings in the 1960's, as well as the commission President Gerald Ford appointed to look at embarrassing new revelations about the misdoings of the CIA. Other commissions seem to have little other purpose than to throw the President's political opposition off-guard—such was one of the purposes of President Lyndon Johnson's Commission on Urban Problems, headed by liberal Paul H. Douglas.[51] However, contrary to the frequent critics of the commissions, the overwhelming majority are meant to suggest new policy initiatives or to build support for programs the President wishes to pursue. This point has been established in a thorough study by political scientist Thomas Wolanin of all commissions appointed between 1945 and 1972, but it is evident from earlier and less systematic accounts as well.[52]

Although several social scientists have recognized the significant policy influence of many presidential commissions, they have

51. Howard E. Shuman, "Behind the Scenes and Under the Rug," *The Washington Monthly*, July, 1969.

52. Thomas R. Wolanin, *Presidential Advisory Commissions* (Univ. of Wisconsin Press, 1975). For accounts of earlier commissions, see Carl Marcy, *Presidential Commissions* (King's Crown Press, 1945). For three informative "case studies" on specific commissions, see Morton H. Halperin, "The Gaither Commission and the Policy Process," *World Politics*, April, 1961; Usha Mahanjani, "Kennedy and the Strategy of Aid: The Clay Report and After," *Western Political Quarterly*, September, 1965; and Daniel Bell, "Government By Commission," *The Public Interest*, Spring, 1966.

failed to grasp the intimate connection between presidential commissions and private policy groups. They merely note that the commissions have representatives from many sectors of society—business, labor, farming, women, minorities and various religious groups—even while acknowledging that there is a considerable bias toward older white males of business and professional occupations.[53] This emphasis on the wide range of people on commissions is of course reinforced by the news media.

Fifteen commissions dealing with aspects of foreign and military policy were established between 1945 and 1972. Twelve were headed by a member of the Council on Foreign Relations; two others were headed by trustees of the Committee for Economic Development. Five commissions were concerned with problems of governmental reorganization and federal salaries; four were chaired by members of the Committee for Economic Development, which has taken a special interest in such matters through its Committee for the Improvement of Management in Government.[54]

The numerous commissions dealing with diverse problems of health, education, urban housing, population, science policy, the status of women, national goals, the patent system, aging and prisoner rehabilitation were more likely to be headed by specialists in the specific field, but even here several of the chairpersons were members of major policy groups.

Because those who have written about commissions do not link them to policy groups, they cannot recognize their most important role, which is to legitimate and make "official" the ideas that have been developed in the private-sector policy net-

53. Frank Popper, *The President's Commissions* (Twentieth-Century Fund, 1970), p. 19. Popper also notes that black women are better represented than white women because they can be said to represent two constituencies.

54. Schriftgiesser, *op. cit.*, chapter 20.

work. It is in the commissions that representatives of labor, minorities, women and other sectors of society are given a chance to participate in the process of policy formation and thereby to become convinced of the sensibleness of the new ideas. Thus, the commissions help give new policies a society-wide stamp of approval as well as official sanction.

One of the most important commissions to play these roles was President Harry Truman's Committee on Foreign Aid, which was appointed in June, 1947 to help formulate the specifics of the Marshall Plan. Chairing the twenty-member commission was Secretary of Commerce Averell Harriman, who had chaired the Business Advisory Council from 1937 to 1939. The rest of the members were private citizens, and were of course advertised as representing major sectors of American life. Strictly speaking, this was true, for there were two labor leaders, two agricultural school representatives and a former liberal Senator (Robert M. La-Follette, Jr.) among the members. However, there also were nine businesspeople, five of whom were trustees of the Committee for Economic Development. Six academic experts served on the commission—three were research advisors to the CED. Another member of the committee was the president of The Brookings Institution. Six members of the committee, including chairperson Averell Harriman, were members of the Council on Foreign Relations.

The commission recommendations followed closely the ideas for implementing a foreign-aid program that had been developed during the previous years by several policy groups. Especially important was the work of a special task force which had representatives from several policy groups and the labor movement.[55]

55. David Eakins, "Business Planners and America's Postwar Expansion," David Horowitz, ed., Corporations and the Cold War (Monthly Review Press, 1969).

Since the ideas behind the plan already were generally agreed upon within CFR-CED circles, the commission's major contribution was to help sell them. This point was clearly recognized by the commission member who was CED president from 1942 until he resigned in 1949 to become the chief administrator of the Marshall Plan:

From a public relations standpoint, I think the work of the Harriman committee was crucial. It was an appraisal with the participation of representatives of business, labor, agriculture, and the public generally. It was well conceived and was taken seriously.[56]

Another highly influential Truman-appointed commission was the Materials Policy Commission, which is credited with bringing about a whole new way of thinking about natural resources and their allocation. As a member of the staff later explained:

It was particularly important in reorienting thinking away from the perspective of professional resource people who saw resources in terms of their uniqueness, and toward an economist's perspective of seeing resources in terms of substitutions and trade-offs rather than absolute limits. It was influential in setting the way to think and talk about the problem.[57]

This new orientation toward natural resources was embodied in a new policy group—Resources for the Future—which has continued to sustain and build support for the economic viewpoint. Indeed, several members and staff from the commission became directors and executives of this new addition to the policy network.

56. Harry B. Price, *The Marshall Plan and Its Meaning* (Cornell Univ. Press, 1955), p. 46n.
57. Wolanin, *op. cit.*, p. 148.

Commissions often succeed in their legitimation of an issue even when they are ignored or rejected by the President. Such was the case of the President's Commission on Population Growth and the American Future. Appointed in 1969 by President Richard M. Nixon at the urging of John D. Rockefeller III, the commission included several members of the population establishment as well as three blacks, a Mexican-American woman, a Puerto Rican and several Catholics. Representatives from these minority and religious groups were considered especially important because of their potential opposition to population-control policies. Members of the commission differed widely in their beliefs about population control, but they came to basically agree on their recommendations. Two of the recommendations were politically volatile—the liberalization of abortion laws and the provision of contraceptive information and services to teen-agers.

The commission released its report in stages to maximize exposure of the whole report and to minimize adverse reaction to the abortion recommendations. In the election year of 1972, Nixon at first ignored the report, then rejected the controversial recommendations. Disappointing as this response was to many commissioners, it did not mean that their work was for naught:

But that is not the case. The report has featured prominently in the activities of at least one congressional committee and has been used in various ways in government departments responsible for family planning, population research and statistics, population education, and other subjects within the subject of population distribution. Perhaps of even greater long-run importance than immediate action by the executive or legislative branches is the educational and the international impact that the report is having and will continue to have.[58]

58. Charles F. Westoff, "The Commission on Population Growth and the American Future," in Mirra Komarovsky, ed., *Sociology and Public Policy: The Case of Presidential Commissions* (Elsevier Scientific Pub. Co., 1975), p. 58.

A detailed study of the relationship between policy groups and all types of presidential commissions remains as one of the many pieces of unfinished business awaiting students of power in the United States. For now, the evidence is clear that the most important and policy-oriented of these commissions are closely related in personnel and ideas to the CFR, the CED and other policy groups. Commissions are an important link in the policy network which have been overlooked by most social scientists.

THE POLICY NETWORK IN ACTION

In describing the major institutions of the policy network, bits and pieces of evidence have been presented which suggest that various policy groups have had great influence in determining one or another government policy on a general issue. However, no major policies have been traced through the entire network in order to demonstrate how the full process operates. This defect will now be remedied by presenting three case studies in different issue-areas. The examples are of necessity historical in nature. This is because the material for in-depth contemporary studies is not readily available. Unlike the more visible special-interest process, which is relatively accessible to the enterprising investigator, the policy process operates in more private channels. The details of its workings only become clear years later when private papers and government documents become available.

THE ORIGINS OF REGULATORY AGENCIES

Social scientists are quite willing to admit that regulatory agencies have been "captured" by the special interests they are

supposed to regulate. That much has become part of the ortho-
doxy. But to let it go at that is to accept a piece of conventional
wisdom that is largely wrong. In that reading of the American
past, so popular among historians, regulatory agencies were
created by strong popular desire and anticorporate reformers.
Only later were they taken over by the clever vested interests.[59]

Contrary to this view, there is good reason to believe that
something more sophisticated and subtle actually happened. An
examination of the papers of the first nationwide policy-planning
group suggests that regulatory agencies were the device used
by probusiness reformers to quell popular agitation and the
proposals of antibusiness reformers and socialists. Corporate
leaders in fact had a comprehensive view of the social system
and the political situation when they became supporters of
regulation. As one of them said in 1909, it is better to "help
shape the right kind of regulation than to have the wrong kind
forced upon [you]."[60]

The first regulatory commission, the Interstate Commerce
Commission, was created in 1887 to regulate railroads. It was
not the product of a policy-planning group; there were none in
existence at that time. However, even the ICC does not signify
the triumph of the popular will over the united opposition of
powerful railroads. Rather, according to the careful research
of historian Gabriel Kolko:

59. E.g., Richard Hofstadter, *The Age of Reform* (Knopf, 1955), pp. 164
and 231; Marver Bernstein, *Regulating Business by Independent Commission*
(Princeton Univ. Press, 1955), pp. 21 and 35. For the most extreme statement, see Theodore Levitt, "Why Business Always Loses," *Harvard Business Review*, March–April, 1968, p. 82, where it is claimed that "Business
has not really won or had its way in connection with even a single piece of
proposed regulatory or social legislation in the last three-quarters of a
century."

60. Weinstein, *op. cit.*, p. 87.

. . . the intervention of the federal government not only failed to damage the interests of the railroads, but was positively welcomed by them since the railroads never really had the power over the economy, and their own industry, often ascribed to them. Indeed, the railroads, not the farmers and shippers, were the most important single advocates of federal regulation from 1877 to 1916. Even when they frequently disagreed with the details of specific legislation, they always supported the principles of federal regulation as such. And as the period advances, this commitment to regulation grew even stronger.[61]

In turning to the federal government for regulation, the railroad leaders were searching for a way to 1) regulate competition within their own industry; 2) protect themselves against shippers who demanded expensive rebates; and 3) avoid the possibility of regulation by a variety of state governments. Kolko stresses that they did not seem to have much concern with the general implications of accepting regulation. They were reacting in a step-by-step manner to the specific problems of their industry. However, business leaders in general soon drew some wider lessons from the railroad experience, and the usefulness of regulation was common knowledge in the corporate community by the early years of the twentieth century:

In proposing the federal regulation of business, advocates of the new Hamiltonianism were quite aware of the advantages such regulation would have in shielding them from a hostile public, as well as in introducing stability and control in economic affairs.[62]

The understanding of the benefits of regulation could have spread through the business world by any number of means,

61. Gabriel Kolko, *Railroads and Regulation, 1877–1916* (Princeton Univ. Press, 1965), p. 3.
62. Gabriel Kolko, *The Triumph of Conservatism* (Free Press, 1963), p. 178.

but there is no question that the process was refined and made direct by the formation of the National Civic Federation in 1900. The federation was the Council on Foreign Relations, Brookings Institution and Business Roundtable of its day. Its model was the Chicago Civic Federation, which had functioned as a business forum on major issues for six years. After leaders in the Chicago group held a successful conference on trusts in 1899, they decided to extend the idea of their organization nationwide. The result was a New York–based organization with leaders from one-third of the three hundred largest businesses of the time.[63] The new federation also employed or attracted as members many of the leading academic reformers of the era, and especially economists. As historian David Eakins demonstrated, the NCF provided the first setting within which the advice of the fathers of present-day social science could be heard and utilized by business leaders.[64]

Most significantly, the federation did not consist solely of businesspeople and academic experts. It also included many of the major union leaders of the day, which was necessary in an organization whose major concern was the improvement of relations between capital and labor. The federation incorporated most of the features of present-day policy groups. It had discussion groups, research task forces, position papers, meetings with government officials and even a journal. The founding of the NCF symbolizes the arrival of a corporate America, for its leaders were as concerned with combating the "anarchists" in the employers'

63. See Gordon M. Jensen, "The National Civic Federation: American Business in an Age of Social Change and Social Reform," unpublished Ph.D. dissertation, Princeton University, 1956, pp. 57–59 and 344, for this and other evidence that the members of the federation were big businesspeople of great wealth.

64. Eakins, op. cit., chapters 1 and 2.

camp as they were subduing the "socialists" in the wage-earners' camp.[65]

One of the major interests of federation leaders was in the creation of regulatory agencies. This is no better demonstrated than in a case study of the Federal Trade Commission Act of 1914. This act led to the establishment of the five-person Federal Trade Commission, which is charged with regulating business for possible violations of rules and regulations having to do with competition, fair trade and antitrust. In the folklore, the FTC was an anticorporation measure instituted by a government intent upon controlling big corporations. Nothing could be much further from the truth. It was businesspeople who wanted federal regulation so there would be no state-level regulation. Most of all, they wanted "an administrative agency ready to sanction anticompetitive action and provide security from possible state or federal trust prosecution—to provide stability and predictability in a politically and economically fluid climate."[66]

After numerous discussions in its first four years concerning the virtues of regulation, the National Civic Federation made its first concerted public effort for regulatory commissions in 1905 when it established a Commission on Public Ownership of Utilities. The chairperson of the commission was also the chair of the board of the Big Four Railroad, which meant that he had considerable experience with a regulatory agency. The task of the commission was to deflate the growing support for public ownership of electric and gas utilities. The idea was "to take the matter out of politics," and to give the attorney general's office "good grounds" to "slack up a little on its prosecutions," according to a letter from the federation executive director to

65. Weinstein, *op. cit.*, p. 11.
66. Kolko, *The Triumph of Conservatism, op. cit.*, p. 132.

one of the most important Republican senators of that era.[67] The work of the commission provided a general framework for future regulatory laws. Its work was used shortly thereafter as a model for a new public utilities commission in Wisconsin, and regulatory agencies designed to oversee public utilities soon made their appearances in other states.

The second significant NCF effort in the field of regulation was its National Conference on Trusts and Combinations in 1907. The conference included many guests who were not NCF members. The recommendations of the conference were generally sympathetic with the objectives of NCF leaders. They included a resolution that Congress establish a special commission to study the feasibility of a regulatory agency for business. When NCF leaders went to Washington to urge the creation of this study commission, congressional leaders countered by requesting that the NCF instead draft a bill which embodied its suggestions.

An NCF committee of businesspeople, corporate lawyers and labor leaders quickly went to work on the new legislation. In addition to the provisions most eagerly desired by big businesspeople, the model bill included a clause which would exempt organized labor from the court harassment it had suffered for alleged antitrust activities under the Sherman Act. Kolko argues, with considerable effectiveness, that the clause favoring unions was the undoing of the act. Its presence led to all-out opposition by the antilabor National Association of Manufacturers and middle-sized business associations which had previously supported the general principle of a regulatory agency for business.[68]

Much of the concern corporate executives felt in urging a

67. Weinstein, *op. cit.*, p. 74.

68. Kolko, *op. cit.*, pp. 135–137. Weinstein, *op. cit.*, p. 80, believes that it was the wide latitude given to big business—not the labor clause—which was opposed by the smaller businesspeople.

regulatory agency for themselves was relieved in 1911 when the Supreme Court ruled that "reasonable trusts" should be allowed to exist. Some thought the court decision made further legislative activity unnecessary. However, leaders within the federation did not agree with this conclusion, and they continued to work on a new bill which had been under discussion in one of their committees since 1909. The new approach was to be modeled after the Interstate Commerce Commission and the British Board of Trade. In October, 1913, when it appeared that such legislation might have a chance of passing, the NCF executive director met with the attorney general, informing him that he had another draft bill that the federation would like to have considered:

The federation's plan provided for a seven-man Interstate Trade Commission chosen by the president and with powers of investigation and subpoena, and the ability to refer its complaints to the courts and fine companies $5,000 for each violation. The commission could license corporations, and would require annual reports. Its jurisdiction would apply to companies with sales of $10 million and up. The proposal received an important circulation [within the government] and a copy was sent to [President] Wilson . . .[69]

Copies of the new bill, which included no provisions to help labor unions, also were sent to Senator Francis G. Newlands of Nevada, a federation member of great personal wealth, and to Representative Henry D. Clayton, chairperson of the House Committee on the Judiciary. About a month after receiving the draft bill, Newlands and Clayton introduced identical bills in the Senate and House on the same day. However, the bills they introduced were somewhat weaker than the NCF bill, and called for a five-person commission instead of seven.[70]

69. Kolko, *op. cit.*, p. 259.
70. *Ibid.*, p. 261.

The legislative struggle that followed produced no surprises. There were arguments over the restriction on interlocking directorates and questions concerning the status of trade unions under the antitrust act. Amendments by the Chicago Association of Commerce and the national-level Chamber of Commerce made the bill somewhat stronger. However, the bill that emerged was very similar to that suggested by the NCF. The new commission had only five members instead of seven, and there were no federal licensing provisions for interstate business, but the federation bill was "almost a model for the final legislation in every other respect."[71] Most members of the federation were very pleased with it. The minutes of its executive committee shortly after passage report with pride that the NCF had had a "profound effect" on Congress.[72] If the act was antibusiness, the federation did not recognize it.

As the corporate leaders had anticipated, the Federal Trade Commission solved a number of their business problems as well as making it easier to ward off political and legal attacks. They were now free to regulate themselves by means of a governmental agency that was safely removed from party politics and court suits. Once the commission was established, the business leaders could concern themselves with who was going to run the agency and how the law was to be interpreted. This is of course where the standard studies of regulatory agencies pick up the story and then lament the failure of legislation that supposedly was meant to "control" big business. The role of policy-planning groups drops from view, and social scientists and historians can write about a fragmented business community that is not capable of planning for its overall interests.

71. Weinstein, *op. cit.*, p. 89.
72. *Ibid.*, p. 90.

SHAPING A NEW WORLD ECONOMY, 1939–1944

Several of the most important features of the international order after World War II—including the International Monetary Fund, the World Bank and the United Nations—were conceived by a small group of planners at the Council on Foreign Relations between the years 1939 and 1942. Working under the auspices of the War and Peace Studies Project, the council developed close ties with the State Department and infused the government with its view of the "national interest" for the postwar era. It was a conception of the national interest which envisioned an integrated world economy with the United States at its center.

As noted earlier, the Council on Foreign Relations is just about everybody's favorite example of an important policy-planning group. However, until a detailed historical study by Laurence H. Shoup and William Minter pieced together the story of the War and Peace Studies Project by searching through a wide variety of private and government documents, there had been no systematic documentation of the council's influence within the government.[73] Their detective work on the War and Peace study groups more than fills this gap, for the council's project provided the framework for thinking on foreign policy for the next thirty years. It was not until America's defeat in Southeast Asia created major economic and political problems for the power elite that its leaders within the area of foreign policy convened new study committees and formed fresh discussion organizations in an effort to rethink the basic assumptions provided by the earlier work of the council.

Immediately after World War II broke out in Europe in September, 1939, leaders within the Council on Foreign Rela-

73. Shoup and Minter, *op. cit.*, chapter 4.

tions began to think about what United States war aims should be. They also were concerned to develop plans for the shape of the postwar world. The executive director of the council and the editor of its magazine, *Foreign Affairs*, traveled to Washington two weeks after the war began to express their concerns to State Department officials and to gain official support for the council's proposal to study these problems. The contact was made easily because of numerous direct links between the council and State, including the close relationship between Council president Norman H. Davis and Secretary of State Cordell Hull.

State Department officials expressed interest in the council plan. They communicated their approval to the Rockefeller Foundation, which had received an application for funding from the council. Two months later, in December, 1939, the foundation gave the council the first of several grants which were to total about $300,000 over a six-year period.[74]

The work of the War and Peace study groups was to involve about a hundred men over the next five years. They included the top bankers, lawyers, businesspeople, economists and military experts of the era. A central steering committee guided the work of five study groups labeled Economic and Financial, Political, Armaments, Territorial and Peace Aims. These groups were to "engage in a continuous study of the course of the war, to ascertain how the hostilities affect the United States and to elaborate concrete proposals designed to safeguard American interests in the settlement which will be undertaken once hostilities cease."[75] The results were to be communicated to the government at regular intervals. Over the years the groups held 362 meetings and

74. *Ibid.*, p. 122.

75. *Ibid.*, p. 120, quoting a Council on Foreign Relations memorandum for December, 1939.

prepared 682 documents for the State Department and the President: "Up to twenty-five copies of each recommendation were distributed to the appropriate desks of the department, and two to the President."[76]

Leaders within the War and Peace study groups also met with the State Department's planners when the department established its own committees for postwar planning. The relationship was especially close with Leo Pasvolsky, the special assistant to the Secretary of State for postwar planning. Pasvolsky traveled to New York to attend meetings of the Economic and Financial group and sometimes met with council leaders when they came to Washington. On May 1, 1940, for example, Pasvolsky met with four of the main principals in the War and Peace studies "in order to coordinate the project's studies still more closely with the State Department's needs and to discuss the Economic and Financial Group's study program."[77]

At first the groups involved themselves in short-term war aims, urging President Roosevelt to apply the Monroe Doctrine to Greenland and to trade fifty destroyers to Great Britain in exchange for naval bases on British possessions. For our purposes here, however, the most important work concerned the council's assessment of the long-term economic needs of the nation. In the summer and fall of 1940, the Economic and Financial group conducted a series of studies on trade balances and surpluses which concluded that the American economy must be linked with the British Empire, Asia and South America if it was to grow and prosper. Anything less would create trade imbalances, insufficient outlets for manufactured goods, and a shortage of raw materials, it was claimed. The result would be

76. *Ibid.*, p. 122.

77. *Ibid.*, p. 125, quoting a progress report by the secretary of the War and Peace studies project for July 3, 1940.

a stagnating economy that would need government intervention and a greater degree of planning than was acceptable to the great majority of the participants in the study groups.[78]

Having defined the national interest in terms of the improved functioning of a free-enterprise economy that had been rescued from a lengthy depression only by rearmament programs, the War and Peace study groups then turned their attention to developing the policies that would ensure United States hegemony in what the council called the "Grand Area." The result was Memorandum E-B19 in October, 1940. Prepared for the President and the Department of State, it was intended "to set forth the political, military, territorial and economic requirements of the United States in its potential leadership of the non-German world area including the United Kingdom itself as well as the Western Hemisphere and Far East."[79] The proposal called for a fast pace of American rearmament, opposition to Japanese expansionism and development of the international economic and political institutions necessary to integrate and protect the Grand Area.

The council returned to the needs of the Grand Area in 1941 with Memorandum E-B34. It reemphasized the need to defend the entire area so that the American economy could function properly. It stressed that the area could serve as an organized nucleus in building a postwar economy. It called for further study of the mechanisms for integrating the Grand Area:

At the end of recommendation E-B34, the Economic and Financial Group outlined the key topics for future study on integrating the Grand Area. Leading the list were financial measures—the creation of international financial institutions to stabilize currencies, and of international banking institutions to aid in investment and development of

78. *Ibid.*, pp. 125–128.
79. *Ibid.*, p. 128, quoting Memorandum E-A10, October 19, 1940.

backward areas. They had thus identified at a very early date the need for the International Monetary Fund and the World Bank, which they were to specifically suggest in February 1942.[80]

When the United States became involved in the war in December, 1941, leaders within the State Department and the council immediately decided to create a special committee on postwar planning within the department. The proposal for this Advisory Committee on Postwar Foreign Policy was drafted by department planner Pasvolsky in consultation with the council president. Its subcommittees—Armament, Political-Territorial and Trade-Financial—corresponded with the structure of the War and Peace study project. Drafting of committee reports would be by government agencies and by "such non-governmental agencies as the Council on Foreign Relations."[81]

The fourteen-member Advisory Committee on Postwar Foreign Policy included eight men who were council members or participants in its War and Peace study groups. Two of the three subcommittees were chaired by council activists. In addition, the research secretaries of the five War and Peace study groups were hired as part-time consultants at the State Department. They were to coordinate the work of the council study groups and the department subcommittees. Council leaders wanted the study groups to have "some sort of semi-official standing, perhaps in an advisory capacity, because without that the regular staff of the Department might feel some inhibitions about dealing with us as I know [Under-Secretary of State Sumner] Welles is prepared to have them do."[82]

The appointment of its research secretaries as department

80. *Ibid.*, p. 139.

81. *Ibid.*, p. 149.

82. *Ibid.*, p. 154, quoting a letter from *Foreign Affairs* editor Hamilton Fish Armstrong to Norman H. Davis, January 16, 1942.

consultants satisfied the council desire for a formal liaison. The secretaries worked for the council groups in the first part of the week, then came to Washington later in the week for meetings of the subcommittees. In this way, they could "carry back to the Council the exact research needs of the Advisory Committee."[83]

Despite the official status accorded the council secretaries within the department, there was some friction with the lower echelons of the regular staff. The assistant chief of the division of special research, Harley A. Notter, complained about the role of council members in memoranda to his immediate superior, Pasvolsky. Finally, in September, 1942, Notter drafted his letter of resignation, giving as one of his reasons:

. . . relations with the Council on Foreign Relations. I have consistently opposed every move tending to give it increasing control of the research of this Division, and, though you have also consistently stated that such a policy was far from your objectives, the actual facts already visibly show that departmental control is fast losing ground. Control by the Council has developed, in my judgment, to the point where, through Mr. [Isaiah] Bowman's close cooperation with you, and his other methods and those of Mr. [Hamilton Fish] Armstrong on the Committee which proceed unchanged in their main theme, the outcome is clear. The moves have been so piecemeal that no one of them offered decisive objection; that is still so, but I now take my stand on the cumulative trend.[84]

By 1942, then, the study groups set up by the council in 1939 had been in effect merged into the State Department as its postwar planning apparatus. Council members sat on the

83. *Ibid.*, p. 156, quoting minutes of the Joint Organization Meetings of the Subcommittees on Political Problems, Territorial Problems, and Security Problems, February 21, 1942.

84. *Ibid.*, p. 160. Notter apparently had second thoughts and did not send the letter. But nothing changed within the department.

department's postwar planning steering committee, headed two of the committee's three subcommittees, and served as part-time consultants to the subcommittees. The line between the allegedly independent state bureaucracy and the private policy-planning groups had become very hazy indeed.

The recommendations of the subcommittee closely paralleled the earlier proposals of the council study groups. The first report of the economic subcommittee emphasized the danger of another world depression and stressed the need for the United States to involve itself in the internal affairs of the most important industrial and raw-material–producing nations.[85] Subsequent recommendations called for the creation of the International Monetary Fund and the World Bank, the specific plans for which were worked out by the Treasury Department and adopted at the Bretton Woods Conference in Bretton Woods, New Hampshire, in 1944.

The subcommittees also urged the creation of the United Nations as an important mechanism for political domination of the international economy. Isaiah Bowman, the council director who headed the department's territorial subcommittee, explained the need quite clearly:

At the Council meeting in May, 1942, he stated that the United States had to exercise the strength needed to assure "security" and at the same time "avoid conventional forms of imperialism." The way to do this, he argued, was to make the exercise of that power international in character through a United Nations body."[86]

The actual planning of the United Nations was in the hands of the Informal Agenda Group created by Secretary of State

85. *Ibid.*, p. 165.

86. *Ibid.*, pp. 169–170, quoting Council Memorandum T-A35, May 20, 1942.

Hull in January, 1943. Five of the six original members were from the council, including Isaiah Bowman. When the group later was expanded, seven of the eleven were either members of the council or part of its War and Peace Studies Project. President Franklin D. Roosevelt followed the advice of the Informal Agenda Group closely, calling its members "my postwar advisers."[87] Although there were modifications in the UN charter proposal in the course of negotiations with other nations at the founding conferences in 1944 and 1945, it was the thinking of the council planners which had shaped the American proposal.

There are numerous other aspects of the postwar world—including the Marshall Plan, the hard-line attitude toward the Soviet Union, and the Vietnam War—which grew out of the basic assumptions that the council planners made into conventional wisdom between 1940 and 1945.[88] However, enough detail has been presented to demonstrate that the council defined the national interest in terms of economic expansion, and then formulated the policies which the government later implemented to realize that vision. If the quintessence of class domination is the ability to translate class interest into the national purpose, then the role of the Council on Foreign Relations in shaping the postwar world reveals class domination in week-by-week detail. It is a domination that was intellectual and political as well as economic. Building on corporate wealth, the council outresearched, outplanned and outworked any of its potential class or governmental rivals. As Shoup and Minter conclude:

87. *Ibid.*, p. 170.

88. For evidence on CFR attitudes toward the Soviet Union during World War II, see Laurence H. Shoup, "Shaping the National Interest: The Council on Foreign Relations, the Department of State, and the Origins of the Postwar World, 1939–1943," unpublished Ph.D. dissertation, Northwestern University, 1974. For the complementary role of the Committee for Economic Development and other policy groups in postwar planning in the years 1942 to 1945, see Eakins, *op. cit.*, chapter 8.

The council's power was unrivaled. It had more information, representation, and decision-making power on postwar questions than Congress, any executive bureaucracy except the Department of State, or any private groups.[89]

Mainstream social scientists like to remind us that there is something unique about the issue-area of foreign policy. Since it is different from the others, perhaps the merger of state and ruling class is more complete in this area than in any other. This should not be taken as a criticism of the ruling-class view, however. It is actually support for it, for in a modern nation-state it is foreign policy above all else that provides the context within which other issues and state functions are discussed.

THE EMPLOYMENT ACT OF 1946

The Employment Act of 1946, which began its legislative career as the Full Employment Act, would have been a major victory for liberals and labor if it had passed in anything close to its original form. As first written, it committed the federal government to a series of concrete programs which would have ensured the economic growth necessary to provide everyone with a job. However, the act that finally passed was a pale imitation of the original measure. The story of how even that pale measure was passed reveals a great deal about the manner in which the struggle between business and the liberal-labor coalition unfolds on a major policy issue.

The original—and most radical—idea behind the full employment bill was to have the federal government underwrite the national investment needed each year to ensure full employment. It would be the task of government to determine what amount was needed each year, then to make available to private industry

89. Shoup and Minter, *op. cit.*, p. 172.

and state and local governments the loans necessary to bring total private and public investment up to the target figure. If the loans were not utilized, then Congress would authorize money for public works and other federal projects.[90]

The men behind these ideas were primarily members or employees of two liberal groups: the earlier-mentioned National Planning Association, made up of progressive businesspeople, labor leaders and farm spokespersons; and the National Farmers Union. They worked closely with friends in the Bureau of Agricultural Economics and the Budget Bureau in formulating their plans. Although the National Planning Association published two reports which supported many of the ideas behind the draft legislation, the organization did not take a stand in favor of the bill. Nor did its business leaders take an active role in pressuring for the bill.[91]

The Full Employment Bill first appeared in print in December, 1944, in a year-end report of the War Contracts Subcommittee of the Senate Committee on Military Affairs. Although it did not commit the government to underwriting capital investment, but only to some form of compensatory spending, it drew immediate editorial fire from the conservative press. The *New York Times, Wall Street Journal* and *Journal of Commerce* quickly condemned it as a deficit-spending measure which would lead to collectivism and governmental domination of society. These editorials were the opening signal that the conservative business community again would be hostile to the idea of government planning and spending within the domestic economy.[92]

After the usual jockeying within the backrooms of the Senate,

90. Stephen K. Bailey, *Congress Makes a Law* (Columbia Univ. Press, 1950), pp. 23–24. Bailey's detailed study of this act is one of the classic legislative case studies in the political science literature.

91. Eakins, *op. cit.*, p. 399.

92. Bailey, *op. cit.*, pp. 54–55.

a revised form of the bill was introduced there in January, 1946. The most significant revision was the elimination of the clause "There are hereby authorized to be appropriated such sums as may be necessary to eliminate any deficiency in the National Budget."[93] With the elimination of authorized spending, and the substitution of language which expressly said that appropriations were not authorized unless Congress passed specific spending provisions for each situation, the act was reduced to a call for analysis and recommendations. The collapse to the center had begun. However, the revised act was still far better than any past legislation on employment, and it was supported by numerous labor and liberal organizations, including the AF of L, the CIO, the NAACP, the National Catholic Welfare Conference, the National Conference of Jewish Women and the National Farmers Union. Support from two small-business groups and the qualified endorsement of two big businesspeople from the CED made it possible for proponents to claim that "small businesspeople" and "enlightened big businesspeople" wanted full employment. But the bill really did not have any significant business support.[94]

With further modifications, the bill breezed through the Senate seven months later by an overwhelming 71–10 vote. Businesspeople invited to testify against it were reluctant to do so because they did not want to be seen as favoring unemployment. A conservative Republican senator was asked to provide opposition witnesses, but failed to do so. Only three of the handful of business witnesses were in fundamental opposition—a vice president from a major New York bank, the president of the National Association of Manufacturers and the executive vice president of the Illinois Manufacturers Association.[95]

93. *Ibid.*, p. 48.
94. *Ibid.*, pp. 76–77.
95. *Ibid.*, p. 107.

But the opponents of the bill were soon to be heard loud and clear. They had decided to focus their attention on the House, with its greater ties to rural and conservative constituencies. Heading the conservative forces were the National Association of Manufacturers, the Chamber of Commerce of the United States and the American Farm Bureau Federation, but they were supplemented by numerous other conservative business organizations. State and local chambers were even more opposed to the act than the national Chamber, and put considerable pressure on individual congressmen through their members.

Spearheading the conservative campaign from behind the scenes was a member of the Du Pont family by marriage, Donaldson Brown. Brown was vice chairman of General Motors and a director of the National Association of Manufacturers. Beginning his efforts in September, 1946, he hired a lawyer and economist to help coordinate the opposition campaign. They worked closely with conservatives in the House in lining up witnesses and preparing testimony. Their work was a "sizeable contribution" to the conservative cause; the conservative congressmen did not have adequate staff assistance of their own, but they "had the assistance of General Motors."[96]

The conservative business efforts stopped the bill cold in the House. When it became clear that even the modified Senate bill could not pass, the result was a substitute bill based upon suggestions submitted by the CED, the Chamber of Commerce and a representative of the Machinery and Allied Products Institute. The fundamental principles of the Senate bill were rejected. In their place was a commitment to a "high" level of productivity and employment in which the government avoided competition with private enterprise.[97]

96. *Ibid.*, p. 138.
97. *Ibid.*, p. 167.

No provisions were made as to how this high level of employment was to be reached. The bill merely called for a yearly economic report to provide suggestions for dealing with threats of inflation or depression that might be on the horizon. The House bill also called for a three-person Council of Economic Advisers to help the President prepare this report. It retained the original bill's provision for a joint congressional committee to monitor the economy and deal with the economic report from the President.

The idea of a Council of Economic Advisers was in good part the product of CED leaders who had worked behind the scenes to bring about what they thought would be a sensible bill. Their suggestions were embodied in a report entitled *Toward More Production, More Jobs and More Freedom*. It was known to the House members who were redrafting the bill, and it was published shortly after the new bill was submitted:

Even before the CED statement was published, advance copies had quietly been circulated on Capitol Hill. One fell into the hands of Will Whittington, a moderate conservative from Mississippi, who was one of the congressmen entrusted with redrafting the bill for the House. . . . Spurred by the CED statement and with the help of others in and out of Congress, Mr. Whittington wrote into the revised draft the sections calling for the present Council of Economic Advisers and the Joint Committee on the Economic Report.[98]

Neither the liberal-labor coalition nor the ultraconservatives liked the substitute measure which came out of the House committee. However, the maneuverings of House moderates and the urgings of the White House made it impossible for the full House to vote on anything but the substitute measure. It passed by an easy 255–126 margin. The final bill that came out of the

98. Schriftgiesser, *op. cit.*, p. 23.

House-Senate conference committee was not substantially different from the House version. Its declaration of purpose contained many of the sentiments of the Senate bill, but the substantive results were only the Economic Report, the Council of Economic Advisers and the Joint Committee. The government was not on record as guaranteeing full employment, nor were the governmental mechanisms mandated which would make it possible to create high employment.

For all the complexity of the legislative process and the behind-the-scenes political machinations, the basic outlines of the battle for the Employment Act of 1946 are the following:

1. Liberal economists and legislative technicians in and around the National Planning Association and the National Farmers Union developed a bill that would have gone a long way toward solving unemployment problems by involving the government in underwriting private investment and providing public works jobs. It would have made the government almost as important in guiding the economy as it is in many Western European capitalist countries. However, the business leaders within the NPA did not endorse or push the bill.

2. Ultraconservative businesspeople, rooted in the large and well-organized Du Pont–related corporate enterprises and working primarily through the National Association of Manufacturers, the American Farm Bureau Federation and various single-issue committees, were able to convince ultraconservatives in the House that the bill should be scuttled. However, it was the ultraconservatives' "uncompromising pressure" which "opened the hole through which the more moderate conservative spokesmen ran."[99]

3. Moderate conservatives, primarily from the Committee for Economic Development, developed substitute measures that fit their conception of the limited role government should have

99. Bailey, *op. cit.*, p. 238.

domestically in maintaining a productive economy. As Schrift-giesser rightly summarizes:

While the National Association of Manufacturers and hundreds of local units of the United States Chamber of Commerce vociferously and expensively fought the full employment bill, CED spoke softly in favor of it. But, as it turned out, it carried the big stick.[100]

4. Labor and its liberal allies from middle-income levels had little other choice than to accept the moderate business bill. They did so reluctantly, with the hope that the bill could be modified in subsequent years to include more of the original provisions and mechanisms. Unfortunately, from their point of view, that hope had not been realized as of 1977.

As has been shown, the initiative for the Employment Act came in good part from private policy groups. So did the moderate modifications. However, this is not the whole story in this partic-ular case. Some of the ideas in the act were embodied in the work of the National Resources Planning Board, a New Deal planning agency within the White House which had been author-ized to recommend long-range plans to the President and Con-gress.[101] Although the board had had little or no impact, it was anathema to a great majority of the business community and to most of the moderates and conservatives in Congress. When it issued in 1943 a particularly bold plan for postwar America, complete with a guarantee of full employment, equal access to education and equal access to health and nutrition, Congress re-acted by abolishing the board and placing responsibility for such postwar planning in the hands of two congressional committees. Significantly, the staff for the Senate committee was The Brook-

100. Schriftgiesser, *op. cit.*, p. 20.
101. Eakins, *op. cit.*, p. 291.

ings Institution; the staff for the House committee was directed by the treasurer of Eastman Kodak, who was also a founding officer of the CED.

Congressional conservatives were determined that the board would not reappear in another guise. In the legislation liquidating the board, it was expressly stated that none of its functions could be transferred to another agency and that no discretionary presidential funds could be used to sustain it. And just to be certain, Congress added another provision:

To make the termination of all the works of the NRPB doubly certain, all its files and records were ordered transferred to the National Archives. "It is doubtful," one liberal New Deal Congressman wrote a few years later, "that there was ever such a thorough job of liquidation since the destruction of Carthage by the Romans after the Third Punic War."[102]

Significant planning within the government had been consigned to the dustbins of history. However, this did not mean that no economic planning whatsoever would take place within the United States. It only meant that what planning there was would take place outside government in organizations directly controlled by the corporations. This fact is made clear in the final version of the Employment Act by the inclusion of an express mandate for the Council of Economic Advisers and the Joint Committee on the Economic Report to utilize the work of "private research agencies."[103] The work of the Committee for Economic Development, The Brookings Institution and similar organizations had been legitimated by an act which began its career as a liberal attempt to build more economic power into the government.

102. *Ibid.*, p. 303.
103. Bailey, *op. cit.*, pp. 231–232.

Countries in postwar Europe developed significant policy and research capabilities within the government, but such was not to be the case in laissez-faire America, which had little or no pressure from a socialist movement within the working class and no statist tradition to draw upon. Thus, the meager planning resources deemed necessary by the power elite were developed outside the government, technically speaking. However, the private policy-planning and research groups are so intertwined with government that it is in reality difficult to tell where "government" ends and "private" begins. Only in terms of the potential for democratic control is there no doubt as to what is private and what is public. The policy groups are strictly private in terms of citizen access, and thus highly insulated from popular control. The great hostility to government on the part of American businesspeople, in part based upon a fear that popular forces will surge up to take control of the government, has led to a policy-planning network outside of government.[104] This network may be unique in the Western world, but we must await systematic comparative studies to be sure.

POLICY CONFLICT IN WASHINGTON

Consideration of these case studies raises the possibility of generalizing about the struggle to enact policy in Washington. There are three major groupings to consider. The first is the CFR–CED–Business Council wing of the power elite, which is rooted in the largest corporations and has great influence in the centrist wings

104. For explanations of business hostility to government, see Domhoff, *Who Rules America? op. cit.*, pp. 152–155; and David Vogel, "Why Businessmen Mistrust Their State: The Political Consciousness of American Corporate Executives," *British Journal of Political Science*, December, 1977.

of both political parties. The second is the NAM–Chamber of Commerce–American Enterprise Institute wing of the power elite, with its economic base in smaller corporations and its political influence among ultraconservative Republicans and Southern Democrats. The third is the loose-knit liberal-labor coalition rooted in the trade unions, middle-income liberal organizations, university communities and the independent wealth of a few rich mavericks; its connections are to the liberal wing of the Democratic Party. The major strength of the CFR–CED conservatives is in the Executive branch through its numerous ties to the White House. The major strength of the ultraconservatives is in Congress. The liberal-labor coalition does not have any major stronghold. When push comes to shove, it has to hope that the moderate conservatives will be on its side.

The leanings of the moderate conservatives usually determine the outcome of any policy struggle. If the CFR–CED wing of the power elite decides to go in the direction of change, it develops a plan, or modifies a plan already developed by the liberals and labor, and then enlists the support of liberals, organized labor and minority group organizations. If the CFR–CED wing decides there is no need for any policy changes, which means it is in agreement with the ultraconservative wing and the power elite is united, then it sits by silently while the ultraconservatives destroy within Congress any suggestions put forth by liberals or labor. In short, the liberal-labor coalition is rarely successful without at least the tacit support of the moderate conservatives within the power elite. The ultraconservatives, on the other hand, are not helpless without the moderates. Due to their strength in Congress, they are often able to delay or alter the proposals put forth by the moderates.

I do not claim that this analysis of the policy struggle will fit each and every new bill of general interest that goes before Congress. However, I do assert that it is accurate for the major issues of the twentieth century—foreign aid, welfare spending, government reorganization, civil rights, population policy, environmental policy, and even to a certain extent labor legislation.[105] It is an analysis which acknowledges conflict over policy enactment, including on some issues conflict within the power elite. At the same time, it shows how the power elite—and especially the moderate core based in the largest banks, corporations, foundations and policy groups—dominates policy making. If it does not depict a united power elite that always gets exactly what it wants, it does describe a power elite that has been able to defend the privileges of the ruling class in the face of every insurgency it has faced. Pluralists like to point out that social security, health-care legislation and other measures signify an important improvement in living conditions for a great many people. While this is true to some extent, the proof of the pudding in terms of power is the ability to maintain the class system that sustains ruling-class privileges and prerogatives. On this score, the ruling class has done very well within the general policy arena.

105. The one issue of any importance I have found which does not fully conform to these generalizations is the National Labor Relations Act of 1935. This act granted unions the right to collective bargaining and protection from corporate strikebreakers. The act found several of its precedents in the work of the National Civic Federation of the Progressive Era, but it was opposed by all policy groups except the liberal Twentieth Century Fund when it was proposed. The moderates within the power elite who supported it were overwhelmingly corporate lawyers, academicians and politicians. For accounts that need to be supplemented by work in New Deal archives, see Domhoff, *The Higher Circles, op. cit.*, pp. 218–249; Ronald Radosh, "The Development of the Corporate Ideology of Organized Labor, 1914–1933," unpublished Ph.D. dissertation, University of Wisconsin, 1967; and Stephen J. Scheinberg, "The Development of Corporation Labor Policy, 1900–1940," unpublished Ph.D. dissertation, University of Wisconsin, 1966.

THE FUNCTIONS OF THE POLICY-PLANNING GROUPS

The information presented in the preceding sections provides a basis for suggesting that the policy-planning groups have several functions within the power elite:

1. They provide a setting wherein members of the power elite can familiarize themselves with general issues in a relaxed and off-the-record setting. This is especially the case with Council on Foreign Relations study groups and luncheons, but it is also true for many sessions of the Committee for Economic Development and the Business Council.

2. They provide a setting where conflicts within the power elite can be discussed and compromised. If it sometimes appears that the corporate rich seem to know automatically their self-interest, the appearance is deceptive, for the agreed-upon policy position usually has been formulated only after many false starts and considerable hesitation. Moreover, there are numerous examples of conflict among policy groups, and in particular between those which represent the biggest of the big business on the one hand, and the run-of-the-mill multimillion-dollar companies on the other.

3. They provide a setting wherein members of the power elite can hear the findings of various academic experts. In some cases, study groups within the policy-planning organizations can be characterized as ongoing seminars or briefing sessions for the corporate rich, with experts doing most of the talking.

4. They provide a framework for commissioned studies by experts on important issues, thereby assuring leaders within the power elite that they have the latest and best information on the subject at hand.

5. They provide an informal training ground for new leadership within the power elite. It is in these organizations that big

businesspeople can determine which of their peers are best suited for service in the government.

6. They provide an informal recruiting ground for determining which academic experts may be suitable for government service, either as faceless staff aides to the numerous lawyers and businesspeople who take Washington positions or as executive-branch appointees in their own right.

All of these functions are important ones. Taken together, they add up to the fact that the ruling class has the institutional capability to develop policies on the major issues facing the social system. That is, the power elite is organized "politically" in the deepest meaning of that term, even though its political organizations are called "apolitical," "bipartisan" and "nonpartisan," in a nation where politics only means the electoral antics of one or another political party.

In addition to their functions within the power elite, the policy-planning groups have at least two major functions for the power elite vis-à-vis the rest of society:

1. These groups legitimate their members as "serious" and "expert" persons capable of government service and selfless pursuit of the "national interest." This is by virtue of the fact that group members are portrayed as giving of their own time to take part in highly selective organizations which are nonpartisan in nature.

2. Through such avenues as books, journals, policy statements, press releases and speakers, these groups influence the "climate of opinion" both in Washington and the country at large. This is a point which will be taken up in Chapter 5, when the ideology process is discussed.

The policy-planning groups, then, are not window dressing or mere social gatherings. They are not without function, even if some social scientists see them as "superficial" in their comprehension of "real" issues. The United States is too large, the economy too diverse, and the issues too complex for a ruling class to maintain itself and prosper without them. Policy groups have been developed throughout the twentieth century because they are needed by those who run the corporate system and the government in Washington.

This information on the policy-planning process has implications for the viewpoints held by pluralists and by Marxists such as Nicos Poulantzas and Claus Offe. First, it provides evidence that many businesspeople, bankers and corporate lawyers concern themselves with more than their specific business interests. Second, it shows that leaders from various sectors of the economy are able to get together to discuss the problems of the system as a whole. This contradicts the notion that the corporate elite is fragmented into trade associations and unable to unite except under unusual circumstances. Third, it suggests that the numerous members of the power elite who are appointed to government are equipped with a general issue-orientation gained from power-elite organizations which are explicitly policy oriented. This undercuts any claim that the corporate leaders who come to government are merely figureheads with little idea of what is really happening. Fourth, it reveals that the academic experts thought by some to be our real rulers are in fact busily dispensing their advice to those who hire them.[106] These experts may be "smarter" than the corporate leaders for whom they work, as some experts privately allege, but the corporate leaders are intelligent enough to ask for the advice they need to keep the system running in a way that is consonant with their values, lifestyle and class inter-

106. Suzanne Keller, in *Beyond the Ruling Class* (Random House, 1964), presents the claim that "strategic elites" have replaced the ruling class because the system is too large and complex for ordinary mortals to manage.

ests.[107] Fifth, it demonstrates that the national government, including the presidency, is reliant on the policy-planning organizations for new policy initiatives. The presidency is not free of the vested interests, as in McConnell's analysis. Nor does it have much "autonomy," as in the theorizing of Poulantzas and Offe. As one former aide to President John F. Kennedy wrote:

On the other hand, relatively few ideas seem to come from within government itself. The contribution of government people is likely to be in detail and in implementation, matters I shall come to shortly. The so-called policy planning staffs of departments and agencies usually serve merely as a conduit for ideas from the outside.[108]

In short, if social scientists were to take the implications of the policy-planning process seriously, they would not be able to agree with Grant McConnell when he downgrades the importance of the Business Council by saying "the really effective participants in business politics are those [organizations] which direct their energies almost wholly to hard, specific matters of immediate economic concern to business firms."[109] Instead, they would say that trade associations are among the most important influences within the special-interest process and that the Business Council, along with the Council on Foreign Relations, Committee for Economic Development, Conference Board and their numerous other counterparts, is one of the Archimedean points of the policy process.

107. Henry Kissinger is one of the experts who expresses this kind of disdain for his corporate sponsors. See Roger Morris, "Servants of the Power Club: The Henry Kissinger Model," *The Nation*, September 15, 1976.

108. Adam Yarmolinsky, "Ideas into Programs," in Thomas E. Cronin and Sanford D. Greenberg, eds., *The Presidential Advisory System* (Harper & Row, 1969), p. 94.

109. McConnell, *op. cit.*, pp. 292–293.

Nor would they be able to agree with Marxists such as Claus Offe, who believes that the "state apparatus," somewhat autonomous from the class struggle swirling around it, formulates overall policies for the ruling class as a whole from within its own agencies and bureaucracies. In Offe's own words, "the common interests of the ruling class are most accurately expressed in those legislative and administrative strategies of the State apparatus which are *not* initiated by articulated interests, that is 'from outside,' but which arise from the State organizations' own routines and formal structures."[110] Instead, they would have to acknowledge that the American "state" is not an independent entity with planning and policy capabilities of its own, but a set of agencies and branches staffed by men and women who are dependent upon a corporate policy network when it comes to new initiatives.

Two general books on power in America written since 1970, when the general outlines of the policy network were first presented, have commented on its usefulness, and they are by elitist theorists.[111] The first, Kenneth Prewitt and Alan Stone's *The Ruling Elites*, acknowledges the importance of the "elite clubs" within the business community, but then explains the attention government pays to their views on the basis of a "perceived mutuality of interest" between corporate leaders and high government officials.[112] Because the giant corporations can have great impact on the functioning of the economy, argue Prewitt and Stone, it is necessary for government officials to have policies which will maintain business confidence and "encourage the large

---

110. Claus Offe, "Structural Problems of the Capitalist State," *op. cit.*, p. 35.

111. For earlier versions, see Domhoff, *The Higher Circles, op. cit.*, chapters 5 and 6; and G. William Domhoff, "How the Power Elite Set National Goals," in Robert Perrucci and Marc Pilisuk, eds., *The Triple Revolution Emerging* (Little, Brown and Co., 1971).

112. Kenneth Prewitt and Alan Stone, *The Ruling Elites* (Harper & Row, 1973), p. 68.

firms to invest, employ large numbers of people, and transact a considerable volume of business with supplier and customer firms."[113] If the government officials did not pursue such policies, the resulting economic unrest might lead to political instability and their removal from office by the electorate.

This type of explanation for cooperation between big business and government is appealing to many theorists. For one thing, it allows for some independence of the political system. Most of all, it explains the role of big business "without resorting to the notion of businesspeople engaging in a surreptitious conspiracy to manipulate or dominate the government."[114] Thus, the influence of corporate-based policy groups "arises naturally from the nature of their constituencies [big corporations] and the nature of the economic system."[115] While there is some truth to this view, it is not as penetrating as it seems, for it does not explain why government officials do not instead seek changes in the economic system by appealing to the voters who elected them. The explanation also flies in the face of the fact that the power elite is directly involved in government in the ways demonstrated in this chapter. It is not a surreptitious and conspiratorial involvement, but it is a direct involvement nonetheless.[116]

Another book from the elitist perspective, Thomas R. Dye's

113. *Ibid.*

114. *Ibid.*, p. 69.

115. *Ibid.*

116. For my critique of those who do view policy planning as a conspiracy, see *The Higher Circles, op. cit.*, chapter 8. Although published in 1970, I think this critique remains a basically accurate analysis for the more recent work by those who now call themselves the conspiratorial right, including the several books by its most articulate and witty spokesperson, Gary Allen, author of *None Dare Call It Conspiracy* (Concord Press, 1971), *The Rockefeller File* ('76 Press, 1976) and *Jimmy Carter, Jimmy Carter* ('76 Press, 1976).

Who's Running America?, sees the implications of the process fully and demonstrates its usefulness in understanding how population policy was created in the 1950's and 1960's.[117] The presentation in *Who's Running America?* also improves upon the original formulation of the network by showing how the mass media fit into the process; it is Dye's modified diagram of the network that was presented earlier in this chapter. His modification provides part of the answer to the unasked question in the Prewitt and Stone book as to why government officials do not seek out nonbusiness constituencies rather than concerning themselves with the needs of corporations. It is because the power elite, through the mass media and other means that will be explored in the following pages, make it difficult to convince the electorate that alternative policies are feasible. Thus, Dye's concern with ideological domination provides a more dynamic explanation for what Prewitt and Stone—and many Marxists as well—see as a "perceived mutuality of interest" between the power elite and those government leaders who are not part of it.

If the analysis presented in this and the preceding chapter is even partially accurate, then it should be clear that most narrow government policies are dominated by specific industries and trade associations within the special-interest process, and that broad-gauge policies are determined by the power elite as a whole through a complex maze of foundations, think tanks and policy-planning organizations. Such a conclusion leads naturally to the obvious question: How is this state of affairs possible in a country wherein government representatives are elected by all of the people, and not just by the wealthy few? Shouldn't it be expected, as many social scientists claim, that parties and politicians have

117. Thomas R. Dye, *Who's Running America?* (Prentice-Hall, 1976), chapter 9.

policy views of their own, and that these policy views generally reflect the wishes of the majority within the electorate who send them to office? The answers to these questions must be sought in the functioning of the candidate-selection process, which is the subject of the next chapter.

4
The Candidate-Selection Process

The candidate-selection process is the means by which elective offices are filled in the United States. It is a process that is often called "political," but it is more preoccupied with individual ambition and image-building than it is with substantive issues. It is a process in which most politicians develop binding ties to one or another clique within the power elite while professing to speak for "the people."

Office-filling in the United States takes place primarily through two political parties. These two parties exist and have the form they do because of the nature of the electoral rules. "Parties and elections are so intertwined," notes political scientist Theodore J. Lowi, "that the very structure of parties is shaped by the electoral process."[1] In the case of the United States, it is the fact of presidential and gubernatorial elections, and the selection of

1. Theodore J. Lowi, *American Government: Incomplete Conquest* (Dryden Press, 1976), p. 265.

legislators from single-member geographical districts, which lead to a two-party system. The election of a single President for the nation, single governors for each state, separately elected senators for each state, and single representatives for each congressional district creates a series of "winner-take-all" contests in which the most sensible strategy is to form the largest possible preelectoral coalition even if numerous policy positions must be abandoned, compromised, or kept hidden from the voters. The result of a winner-take-all system is two political parties, and only two political parties, because a vote in favor of a third party actually is a vote for the person's least-desired choice.

By way of contrast, the electoral rules of most democratic countries create a different party system, for they have a parliamentary rather than a presidential structure. Because the Prime Minister is selected by the legislature from among its members after the election, there is less pressure toward two preelectoral coalitions, thus making the existence of several issue-oriented parties possible. Even more parties are likely to exist if the parliament is elected by a system of proportional representation, giving each party legislative seats roughly proportional to the percentage of the entire electorate which supports it. According to sociologist Seymour M. Lipset, "every country which uses proportional representation has four or more parties represented in the legislature, and, except in Norway, Sweden, and Ireland in recent decades, absolute parliamentary majorities of one party have been extremely rare."[2]

Comparative studies of the relationship between electoral rules and the number of political parties show quite clearly why candidate selection in the United States is through a two-party system

2. Seymour M. Lipset, *The First New Nation* (Basic Books, 1963), p. 336. For a discussion of the various types of proportional representation systems, see Douglas W. Rae, *The Political Consequences of Electoral Laws* (Yale Univ. Press, 1967).

despite the existence of the same class, regional and ethnic conflicts that have led to three or more parties in other countries. Lipset summarizes the results of these studies:

If enough cases existed for analysis, the following rank-order correlation might be found between electoral systems and the number of political parties: presidential systems with single-member districts and one plurality election—two parties; parliamentary system with single member districts and one plurality election—tendency to two parties; parliamentary system with single-member districts and alternative ballot or run-off (second) election—tendency to many parties; proportional representation—many parties.[3]

The two-party system produced in the United States by its unique electoral system is seen by many social scientists as a major bulwark of pluralism. Its very existence is thought to contradict the notion of dominance by a ruling class or power elite. According to this view, the competition between the two parties leads politicians who desire office to adopt and work for the policy alternatives preferred by the majority of voters. Parties and their candidates are said to be primarily interested in one thing, and only one thing: winning elections and holding office. As in laissez-faire economic theory, selfish competition leads to a result that is good for society. Economist Donald A. Wittman, who is skeptical about this traditional model, summarizes it as follows:

Selfishness and competition by the parties are shown to lead to an optimal result. Adam Smith's "Invisible Hand" has been applied to politics.[4]

3. *Ibid.* For the first full presentation of this argument in relation to the United States, see E. E. Schattschneider, *Party Government* (Holt, 1942).
4. Donald A. Wittman, "Parties as Utility Maximizers," *The American Political Science Review*, June, 1973, p. 491.

Representative of this typical pluralist view of the parties is the analysis by political scientists Nelson W. Polsby and Aaron B. Wildavsky of the way in which the presidential election limits and shapes national policy. They begin by stating the argument in its most general form:

The two political parties to a certain extent act as transmission belts for policy preferences in the general population. They perform this function partly out of choice—as partisans, party leaders know more and care more about issues—but mostly out of necessity.[5]

Polsby and Wildavsky stress that the fear of losing office keeps politicians responsive to the voters: "In a competitive two-party system such as exists in American presidential politics, the lively possibility of change provides an effective incentive for political leaders to remain in touch with followers."[6] At the same time, the authors emphasize that there is no direct relationship between the policy preferences of voters in a single election and the behavior of the President in office. For a variety of reasons, they say, "there are few clear mandates in our political system owing to the fact that elections are fought on so many issues and in so many incompletely overlapping constituencies."[7] Thus, it takes time for the relationship between policies and elections to work itself out: "Aside from casting extremists out beyond the pale, free elections and a two-party system operate to bring governmental policy roughly in line with intense public preferences over a reasonable span of time."[8]

Polsby and Wildavsky contrast their pluralist view with what

5. Nelson W. Polsby and Aaron B. Wildavsky, *Presidential Elections*, second ed. (Charles Scribner's Sons, 1967), p. 269.

6. *Ibid.*, p. 273.

7. *Ibid.*, p. 275.

8. *Ibid.*, p. 280.

they think to be a power-elite perspective: "A cynical view would hold that the United States was ruled by a power elite—a small group outside the democratic process."[9] The fatal misconception in their characterization of the power-elite position is in the phrase "outside the democratic process." If there is anything to a power-elite or ruling-class analysis of the United States, it is in its ability to show how the power elite operates within—not outside—the democratic process, including the two-party system.

The two-party system does not operate in the way that is suggested by Polsby, Wildavsky and other pluralists who adopt the analogy between business firms competing in the marketplace for consumers and political parties competing in the electoral arena for voters. First, there is considerable evidence that neither party has responded to the policy preferences of the majority of voters, who are much more liberal on economic issues than either of the parties.[10] This suggests that party leaders and their candidates have some policy preferences of their own, a fact which undercuts one of the basic assumptions of the pluralist argument.[11]

Nor do the parties always try to win, as they are supposed to do according to the pluralists. There are numerous examples where party leaders have preferred to lose with a candidate who shared their views rather than win with one who seemed to be more popular with the electorate. Such was the fate of populistic Democratic candidates in the Midwest in the late nineteenth century, for example.[12] It also was the fate at the

9. *Ibid.*, p. 274.

10. Richard Hamilton, *Class and Politics in the United States* (Wiley, 1972), chapter 1, brings together the arguments and evidence against the unexamined assumptions of those pluralists who believe the two-party system is responsive to voter preferences.

11. Wittman, *op. cit.*, p. 490.

12. Horace Samuel Merrill, *Bourbon Democracy of the Middle West: 1865–1896* (Louisiana State Univ. Press, 1953).

Democratic National Convention in 1968 of antiwar candidate Eugene McCarthy, who was brushed aside even though polls showed he would do much better against either Nixon or Rockefeller than would Humphrey.[13] Then too, there is evidence that the parties sometimes collude rather than compete. This is especially the case when an "unacceptable" candidate wins the nomination in one or the other of them. For instance, much of the party leadership in California worked against its candidate when socialist Upton Sinclair won the Democratic primary for governor in 1934 with 51 percent of the vote.[14] In 1972, to use an example closer to memory, Southern Democrats and labor Democrats openly or tacitly supported Nixon against the party's candidate, George McGovern. To reciprocate this support, "more than a hundred Republican candidates for seats held by Southern and labor-backed Democrats were simply written off by White House strategists."[15]

Collusion need not be explicit, however. Wittman makes this point after showing through a game-theory argument that collusion between the two parties often makes better sense for them than competition if they are interested in rewards other than winning, as indeed they are:

Although there may be explicit agreements (such as between the Conservatives and Liberals in Colombia), it is much more likely that

13. Wittman, *op. cit.*, p. 494.

14. Upton Sinclair, *I, Candidate for Governor, and How I Got Licked* (End Poverty League, Inc., 1934); Russell M. Posner, "A. P. Giannini and the 1934 Campaign in California" (Bancroft Library, Univ. of California, Berkeley, n.d.); Arthur M. Schlesinger, Jr., *The Politics of Upheaval* (Houghton Mifflin, 1960), pp. 119–121.

15. Walter D. Burnham, "American Politics in the 1970's," in William N. Chambers and Walter D. Burnham, eds., *The American Party Systems*, second ed. (Oxford Univ. Press, 1975).

collusion is implicit. The parties may find many ways of restricting competition with each other: bipartisanship, promotion of mutually acceptable ideologies, marginal changes in the previous administration's policies, and recruitment of those who are not antagonistic to the other party. Even the belief in the impossibility of certain platforms being able to win the election may be a form of implicit collusion if there is more fiction than substance to the belief. Thus the parties compete more *with* the voters than *for* the voters or *with each other*.[16]

Even when an American party adopts the policy positions of a majority of voters, there is no mechanism which ensures that it will carry through with its promises when it assumes office. Once in office, the party has fairly wide discretion to do as it pleases. It can interpret its mandate just about any way it wants to interpret it. Lyndon B. Johnson's landslide in 1964 obviously involved his professions of a less "warlike" policy for Southeast Asia than Barry Goldwater seemed to have, but he and his party escalated the war soon after his victory into the most destructive and murderous attack on a small country that could be imagined short of nuclear bombardment.

For all of these reasons, the major effect of the two-party system in the United States is that it discourages policy discussion, political education and an attempt to satisfy majority preference, rather than encouraging them. It helps to create the confusion and disinterest for which pluralists constantly scold the general public. It leads to campaigns in which there are no issues but personality even when voters are extremely issue conscious. Thus, a Richard M. Nixon can unctuously claim he is dealing with the issues in the 1972 campaign when even a columnist for *The Wall Street Journal* has to remind him that all he does is

16. Wittman, *op. cit.*, p. 498. Italics in the original.

wave the American flag and accuse people who disagree with him of being traitors.[17] Then, after the election, his press secretary can calmly admit that Nixon's second-term policy of large-scale cuts in domestic spending programs was purposely hidden during the campaign:

Why did President Nixon fail to mention during the 1972 campaign that he planned the cuts in domestic programs that have raised such a storm this year? Herbert Klein, the soon-to-depart White House communications director, says frankly that such a tactic would have been "naive—you don't raise unnecessary issues in the middle of a Presidential campaign."[18]

Indeed, you don't raise any issues if you can help it, as the 1976 presidential campaign graphically shows. This was the basic strategy of Jimmy Carter, beginning with the Democratic primaries. He tried to speak in vague generalities and give everyone the impression that he agreed with their viewpoint. He tried to show he was comfortable with ordinary people, and his favorite line was to knock government while complimenting them: " 'I want a government,' he would intone to his rapt audiences in a quiet, deliberate cadence, 'that is as good, and decent, and truthful, and fair, and competent, and idealistic, and compassionate, and as filled with love as are the American people.' "[19]

Most of all, Carter tried to emphasize his personal qualities, especially his trustworthiness. He told people he would never lie to them, even while journalists who followed his campaign closely were amazed by how fast he could forget what he had

17. James P. Gannon, "Is GOP Campaign Rhetoric Too Hot?" *The Wall Street Journal*, September 8, 1972, p. 8.

18. "Post-Election Candor," *Newsweek*, March 26, 1973, p. 15.

19. Jules Witcover, *Marathon: The Pursuit of the Presidency, 1972–1976* (Viking Press, 1977), p. 198.

said a few weeks or months earlier. During the primaries, for example, he told federal government workers at a press conference in Washington, "I'm not anti-Washington, I've never made an anti-Washington statement." A reporter who followed him for the entire campaign wrote:

It was a hard observation to swallow from the never-lie, never-mislead candidate who in a radio ad in Pennsylvania two weeks earlier had been saying: "We know from bitter experience that we're not going to get the changes we need simply by shifting around the same group of Washington insiders. They sit up in Congress every year making the same political speeches and the same unkept promises."[20]

Contrary to the Carter image, one veteran speech writer left the campaign because he found it so deceitful. When he was finally tracked down by enterprising journalists, he reluctantly told them:

The candidate and the campaign were the opposite of what they appeared to be. Instead of being honest and straightforward, there was a degree of manipulation and deception I had not encountered in any other campaign.[21]

Although he knew it would end his career in Washington if he broke the unwritten code and spoke to reporters, the speech writer was too shocked to restrain himself because of the pious image Carter presented in contrast to other politicians: "What made it hard was to listen to the stump speech: 'I will never lie to you; I will never mislead you,' said with fervor and passion, and seeing people believe it."[22] The issues on which the speech

20. *Ibid.,* p. 336.
21. *Ibid.,* pp. 324–325.
22. *Ibid.,* p. 320.

writer found Carter misleading on the basis of his private ob-
servations ranged from defense spending to mass transit to
black-lung benefits for coal miners.

The contrast between campaign speeches and issue reality
was highlighted in a *Wall Street Journal* article that compared
Carter's populist rhetoric with his real attitudes toward big
business. In his acceptance speech at the Democratic National
Convention the candidate inveighed against the "political and
economic elite," noting that their children go to "exclusive private schools." He assailed the "unfair tax structure" that only
serves the needs of this "elite," and he called for "major investments in people and not in buildings and weapons." A week
later, however, he was singing a different tune to fifty corporate
executives at the exclusive "21" Club in New York, assuring
them that he would consult with business on tax changes, and
in general would depend on corporate leaders "very heavily" if
he attained office.[23]

The contrast in the two speeches led *The Wall Street Journal*
to ask "What is Jimmy Carter's real attitude toward business?"
Interviews with those who knew him well convinced the inter-
viewers that business had nothing to fear except a somewhat
stiffer attitude on consumer protection, energy and taxation
than had been evident in the overly generous Nixon and Ford
regimes. Subsequent events were to prove the *Journal* correct.
As Irving S. Shapiro, chairman of Du Pont Corporation and the
Business Roundtable, explained to reporters after a Carter out-
burst against the oil and gas companies in 1977, "it was not
unique for a Democratic president to go after industry, pointing
to similar incidents under Presidents Kennedy and Johnson."
Shapiro told a breakfast meeting of financial writers that "If

23. Albert R. Hunt, "Carter and Business," *The Wall Street Journal*,
August 12, 1976, p. 1.

you're realistic about Washington, you have to expect that these kinds of episodes are going to come and then pass."[24]

If Carter's campaign for the Democratic nomination was one of image-building and issue-avoiding, the general election contest between Carter and Ford was little different. Both candidates focused on the question of "trust," asking voters to put their trust in them on the basis of their personal qualities. Both claimed they were concerned with issues, but both parties concentrated on the personal peccadilloes of the other candidate:

It had not been what one would call an uplifting campaign for the highest elective office in the land. The political horizon had been cluttered with superficial matters: the valances in Clarence Kelley's apartment built by FBI carpenters; artful dodging by both Ford and Carter on the abortion issue, in blatant courtship of the Catholic vote; reports of Ford's free golfing trips (from U.S. Steel) and Carter's (free) hunting trips (from lumber companies); Carter's dissembling on a tax-reform statement and Ford's dissembling on Carter's dissembling; disclosure that Carter lusted in his heart, and pious denunciation from presumably lustless Republicans . . .[25]

Although Carter tried to emphasize personal qualities as much as possible, and hedged on social issues like abortion which tend to split the traditional Democratic constituency, he had to make explicit promises on the kind of populist and economic issues which bring that constituency together. However, he introduced these necessary issues into the campaign only to renege on his promises once he took office. He promised new faces from outside the usual establishment circles, but then appointed the same old insiders from the Council on Foreign Relations and

24. Jack Egan, "Jordan Called Connection Between Business, Carter," the Washington *Post*, October 19, 1977, p. 33.

25. Witcover, *op. cit.*, p. 609.

The Brookings Institution as White House advisors and Cabinet officials.[26] He promised to cut defense spending by $5 to $7 billion, but soon after the election he explained why that couldn't be done, and added that in any case he had only meant he would cut waste by roughly that amount.[27] He promised to cut unemployment to 4–4½ percent by 1980, but at his second press conference after the election he explained that it would not drop gradually to that level, but would remain high for the first four years of his administration.[28] During his campaign Carter waxed eloquent against arms sales overseas, and even after he took office he vowed to reduce weapons sales. "But," reported Newsweek, "like other Presidents before him, Carter has found that hard to do; and at last week's press conference, he found himself defending a flurry of announcements of contemplated arms deals with at least six nations . . ."[29]

The accounts of other recent presidential campaigns do not differ in their conclusions from the Carter-Ford campaign of 1976. They reveal these campaigns as media events in which the excitement and interest are in a kind of person-to-person combat more akin to a sporting match than anything written in social science textbooks about the policy-related functions of politics.[30] In none of these accounts of actual presidential campaigns is there any evidence of serious efforts to learn the concerns of voters and to develop policies to respond to those con-

26. "Mr. Outside Opts for 'Ins'," Newsweek, January 3, 1977, p. 40.

27. "First, A Word of Caution," Newsweek, January 10, 1977, p. 14; "Shakedown Cruise for the Carter Crew," Time, January 10, 1977, page 8.

28. "Carter Sees Jobless Rate of 5 to 7 Pct. for Years," San Francisco Chronicle, November 16, 1976, p. 1.

29. "Carter as Arms Merchant," Newsweek, August 8, 1977, p. 31.

30. E.g., Joe McGinniss, The Selling of the President (Trident Press, 1969); Theodore White, The Making of the President (Atheneum, 1973).

cerns. Rather, the whole emphasis is on manipulation and impression management, tasks made easier perhaps by the hordes of pollsters, media consultants, advance men and other image-creating advisors hired by both parties. Most observers of these campaigns, painfully aware that reality flies in the face of the textbook wisdom, try to retrieve the situation by saying the campaigns at least test the "character" of the candidates under "stress" or "fire." Aside from the fact that such huckstering campaigns probably drive out people who would make good Presidents, this thin rationalization about testing character through running the gauntlet hardly covers for the political emptiness of presidential campaigns.

Systematic studies by political scientists have demonstrated that there is an equally meager relationship between political campaigns and policy issues at the less glamorous congressional level. Most significantly, they have found that there is little or no relationship between the issue preferences of the majority of voters and the policy stands of incumbents running for reelection. Even at this level, campaigns are more image oriented than issue oriented, particularly in the case of incumbents, whose primary effort is to portray themselves as thoughtful, sincere and concerned. Political scientist Charles O. Jones summarizes the results of studies by himself and others as follows:

The major proposition [i.e., conclusion] is that the campaign and election are regularly scheduled events in the political life of a representative in which he makes an intensive effort to project an image of himself as a capable representative—which image is "issue-involved" in that it provides clues as to what to expect by way of policy making behavior from the Congressman. Elections are not primarily policy or issue events where issues are discussed or resolved or where there is an exchange between constituency and candidate. When the representative is returned to office, he is relatively unbound by the campaign and election in his policy making behavior (though he is bound by other factors not measured here).[31]

Contrary to the pluralists, then, American political parties do not involve citizens in the influencing of public policy to any great extent. Candidates are relatively free to say one thing and do another.[32] The major conclusion about the political results of the two-party system as it functions in the United States should be that of Lowi, not the pluralists:

Majorities produced by the American two-party system are simply numerical majorities; they usually have no political content whatsoever.[33]

According to comparative studies of political parties around the world, fully-developed political parties fulfill four major functions: 1) integrating conflicting regional, ethnic and class identifications; 2) selecting candidates to fill offices; 3) political education; and 4) policy making. In the United States, as has been shown, the parties have little or nothing to do with political

31. Charles O. Jones, "The Role of the Campaign in Congressional Politics," in M. Kent Jennings and L. Harmon Zeigler, *The Electoral Process* (Prentice-Hall, 1966), p. 37. According to Jones, the legislator is bound by the groups that have access to him, by his legislative party, by his colleagues on committees with him, and by his "perception" of his constituency and its wishes. Since our perceptions are often dictated by our own wishes and social background, I would argue that the policy influences on the legislator come from an encased world that does not include the general electorate.

32. Witcover, *op cit.*, p. x, reports that a 1976 study of nonvoters, a group which makes up about half of the voting-age population, found that 68 percent of them say they don't bother to vote because "candidates say one thing and do another."

33. Lowi, *op cit.*, p. 299.

education or policy making. "Particularly in our own century," writes political scientist Walter D. Burnham, "American political parties have been largely restricted in functional scope to the realm of the constituent [integrating conflicting regional, ethnic and class identifications] and to the tasks of filling political offices."[34] The executive director of a congressional watchdog organization, the National Committee for an Effective Congress, puts the matter even more strongly:

For all intents and purposes, the Democratic and Republican parties don't exist. There are only individuals [i.e., candidates] and professionals [i.e., consultants, pollsters, dirty tricksters, media advisors].[35]

It is precisely because the candidate-selection process has become increasingly individualistic over the past several decades, and therefore dependent on name recognition and personal image, that it can be in good part dominated by members of the ruling class through the relatively simple and direct means of large campaign contributions. In the guise of fat cats and money raisers, the same men who direct corporations and take part in policy groups play a central role in the careers of most politicians who advance beyond the local level or state legislatures in states of any size and consequence: "Recruitment of elective elites remains closely associated, especially for the more important offices in the larger states, with the candidates' wealth or access to large campaign contributions."[36] Moreover, the role of the

34. Walter D. Burnham, "Party Systems and the Political Process," in Chambers and Burnham, *op. cit.*, p. 279. It is because American politics is restricted largely to office-filling functions that it is most accurately described as a candidate-selection process rather than a political process.

35. John S. Saloma III and Frederick H. Sontag, *Parties* (Knopf, 1972), p. 295.

36. Burnham, *op. cit.*, p. 277.

wealthy donor and the fund raiser seems to be especially crucial in the nomination phase of the process. This was the conclusion of one of the earliest systematic studies of campaign finance:

The necessity for obtaining essential election funds has its most profound importance in the choosing of candidates. The monies can usually be assured, and often can be withheld, by the relatively small corps of political specialists whose job it is to raise money. . . . As a consequence, money probably has its greatest impact on the choice of public officials in the shadow land of our politics where it is decided who will be a candidate for a party's nomination and who will not be. There are many things that make an effective candidate, but here is a *choke point* [my italics] in our politics where vital fiscal encouragement can be extended or withheld.[37]

This conclusion, based on research conducted in the 1950's, is backed up by the experience of the 1960's and 1970's, when the increased use of television, polling, computerized mailings and political consultants made campaigning even more expensive: "Because of its ability to buy the kinds of services that produce name recognition and exposition of positions, money wields its greatest influence on campaigns—particularly presidential races —during the prenomination period."[38]

Although reliable data were hard to come by in the past, the role of big money in major elections has been known to the political scientists who study campaign finance for some time, both through systematic studies and dramatic examples. In 1948, for example, 69 percent of the monies collected by national-level Democratic committees came from individual donations of $500 or more. The percentage was the same in 1964, and it rose even

37. Alexander Heard, *The Costs of Democracy* (Doubleday, 1962), p. 34.
38. Herbert E. Alexander, *Financing Politics* (Congressional Quarterly Press, 1976), p. 44.

higher in 1968.[39] Making the point even more clearly were the 43 people who loaned the 1968 Democratic presidential campaign at least $3.1 million, only part of which was ever paid back. In that election, "at least one half, and perhaps more, of Humphrey's general election campaign expenses were paid for through contributions and loans from about 50 individuals."[40]

However, it was left for the 1972 election to reveal the full scope of large campaign donations. New disclosure laws passed in 1971, combined with the uncovering of various scandals, including Watergate, led to more complete information on campaign financing than ever had been available in the past. The results were stunning. The number of people known to have given $500 or more soared from 15,000 in 1968, when reporting laws were still lax, to 51,000 in 1972. Those known to have contributed $10,000 or over rose from 424 to 1,250. The donations of the $10,000-and-over givers were awesome—these 1,250 individuals gave $51.3 million to national-level candidates. This figure compares rather impressively with the $8.5 million which organized labor donated to all presidential and congressional candidates in 1972, and to the $10.5 million which McGovern netted from 600,000 people in his widely publicized direct mail solicitations in 1971 and 1972.[41]

Large campaign donors are often hard to distinguish in their outlooks, whatever their political party. What differences they do have reflect the conflicts between moderate conservatives and ultraconservatives within the power elite described in the previous chapter. Indeed, many of the largest donors give to both

39. *Ibid.*, p. 69; Herbert E. Alexander, *Financing the 1968 Election* (Heath Lexington Books, 1971), p. 147.

40. Alexander, *Financing the 1968 Election, op. cit.*, p. 152; Alexander, *Financing Politics, op. cit.*, pp. 70–71.

41. Alexander, *Financing Politics, op. cit.*, pp. 71, 86, 90–91 and 106.

parties. In 1972, for example, 36 percent of the $10,000-and-over donors gave to candidates of both political parties. Most of these split-givers were contributing to the presidential campaign of one party and a senatorial or House campaign of the other, but there were also 14 such donors who gave to both Nixon and McGovern.[42] Whatever the motivation for these split gifts, they help to give members of the power elite access to both political parties.

Then, too, members of the major policy discussion groups give to both parties. In 1968, for example, there were 144 members of the Council on Foreign Relations who gave $500 or more to Republican candidates, 56 who contributed $500 or more to the Democrats. Among the trustees of the Committee for Economic Development, there were 95 Republican donors and 16 Democratic donors.[43] The donations of Business Council members have been used by political scientist Herbert E. Alexander as a guide to the political preferences of the top leaders within the corporate community. In 1956 and 1960, over 90 percent of the council members giving $500 or more favored the Republican Party. In 1964, when ultraconservative Barry Goldwater led the GOP, 36 members gave $87,000 to the party, but 33 gave even more—$135,000—to the Democrats. For the 1972 elections, 89 members provided $1 million to the Republicans; 23 gave $154,000 to various Democratic candidates.[44]

Although both parties depend on large donors for a substantial percentage of their funds, a great majority of the corporate leaders clearly prefer the Republicans. The notable exceptions to this rule, of course, are Texans and other Southern-

---

42. *Ibid.*, pp. 85–86.

43. G. William Domhoff, *Fat Cats and Democrats* (Prentice-Hall, 1972), pp. 151 and 154.

44. Herbert E. Alexander, *Financing the 1972 Election* (Lexington Books, 1976), p. 386.

ers. They have been solidly Democratic except in some presidential elections since the late 1870's. At that time they abandoned tentative plans to join the Republicans because the rise of the populists in the late 1870's and 1880's made it clear that the Democratic Party must be kept out of the hands of insurgents by disenfranchising blacks and continuing to scapegoat the Republican Party.[45]

The other major exception to the rule has been among Jewish businesspeople, at least half of whom support the Democrats, providing about half of the party's national-level funds.[46] The reasons for the greater allegiance of Jewish millionaires to the Democratic Party are several, but they do not involve major differences with other big businesspeople on economic issues. According to Stephen D. Isaacs, a Washington *Post* bureau chief in New York, who conducted interviews with dozens of Jewish donors, their major motivation for political involvement is that "it" could happen here.[47] Since ultraconservative Republicans have been a significant source of overt anti-Semitism, the Democratic Party has been a more congenial home for most Jews since at least the New Deal, when Franklin D. Roosevelt and other patrician moderates began to forge a more ethnically representative ruling coalition within the power elite, which included Catholics like Joseph P. Kennedy, Mormons like Marriner S. Eccles, and Jews like Henry Morgenthau, Jr., Herbert Lehman and Felix Frankfurter.[48] As Isaacs summarizes:

45. C. Vann Woodward, *Reunion and Reaction* (Doubleday, 1956); Dewey Grantham, Jr., *The Democratic South* (Univ. of Georgia Press, 1963).

46. Domhoff, *op. cit.*, p. 62; Stephen D. Isaacs, *Jews and American Politics* (Doubleday, 1974), p. 6.

47. Isaacs, *op. cit.*, p. 15.

48. See E. Digby Baltzell, *The Protestant Establishment* (Random House, 1964), for an excellent account of the gradual change in the ethnic composition of the "establishment" since the New Deal.

Jews did not forget and have not forgotten that it was the Republican Party that harbored the anti-Semites in the '20s and '30s, the Republican Party that was home to those who called the New Deal the "Jew Deal," that it was Republicans who made up the majority of the membership of New York's Colony Club, where Mrs. Henry Morgenthau had been snubbed, a famous incident that caused Eleanor Roosevelt to cancel her membership.[49]

In addition to the donations provided directly to candidates, wealthy individuals also support both parties through their contributions to the numerous political action committees of specific corporations and general business organizations. When all of these direct and indirect gifts are combined, the power elite can be seen to provide the great bulk of the financial support to both parties at the national level, far outspending the unions and middle-status liberals within the Democrats, and the mélange of physicians, dentists, engineers, real-estate operators and other white-collar conservatives within the right wing of the Republican Party. Even within the Democrats, the financial weight of the wealthy is overwhelming. Organized labor provided only $7.1 million at the national level in 1968 and $8.5 million in 1972, with most of that going to senatorial and House campaigns.[50] Seldom is labor able to involve itself in Democratic presidential primaries. It does make indirect contributions to the Democrats in the general presidential election through "nonpolitical" efforts such as voter-registration drives, get-out-the-vote campaigns and the printing of "educational" leaflets containing the voting records of Democratic and Republican candidates, but this has not been enough to gain a major voice within presidential politics. Contrary to ultraconservative propaganda, the unions

49. Isaacs, *op. cit.*, p. 156.

50. Alexander, *Financing Politics, op. cit.*, pp. 106–107.

have not been able to come close to matching the television advertising, printed pamphlets and campaign workers that the corporate rich have been able to buy for their candidates in both parties. Even the vaunted CIO Political Action Committee, which functioned from 1944 to 1955, had much less impact than has been attributed to it.[51]

THE EFFECTS OF CAMPAIGN FINANCE REFORM

The central role played by heavy money is a constant strain on the legitimacy of the electoral system. It contributes to cynicism about politics and to a widespread belief that politicians are corrupt and easily bought. This cynicism, combined with the increasing costs of campaigns, has led to reform movements that attempt to decrease the impact of large donations. The success of these reforms is open to question, however.

The upsurge of interest in campaign-finance reform began before Watergate, but was given a tremendous boost by it. Financing laws changed at the national level four times in the first six years of the 1970's. Moreover, 49 states revised regulations on campaign finance between 1972 and 1976.[52] The reforms at both the state and national levels have increased public disclosure of campaign donors, established commissions to monitor campaign spending and placed limits on how much candidates can spend. At the national level, donors are limited to $1,000 per candidate each year. Matching funds are provided for aspirants in presidential primaries who can raise $20,000 in amounts up to $250

51. James C. Fester, *The Union Politic: The CIO Political Action Committee* (Univ. of Missouri Press, 1975).

52. Alexander, *Financing Politics, op. cit.*, pp. 2–3.

per donor in each of 20 states. In addition, public funding is available for the general presidential election, and the national nominating conventions of the two major parties are now subsidized by the government.

Some of these reforms are the products of middle-income insurgents. Others of them, such as full public disclosure, have been urged by moderates within the power elite. In 1968, for example, the Committee for Economic Development advocated several major changes in campaign financing, including tax credits to encourage small donors, stringent disclosure requirements and federal subsidies to public television stations for political presentations.[53]

The new laws will have several effects on fund-raising strategies, but they are unlikely to lessen the role of big money in electoral politics. The reforms will not do away with the need for wealthy fund raisers who can bring together hundreds of friends for a $1,000-a-plate breakfast or dinner. If anything, the role of these essential mediators between the ruling class and political candidates will increase, for it is no longer possible for a few dozen people to finance an entire campaign. Instead of 40–50 percent of corporate directors making large contributions, as has been the case in the past, now it will be necessary for everyone in the corporate community to be dunned more systematically.

A 1976 Supreme Court decision, *Buckley* vs. *Valejo*, a suit brought by a coalition of liberals, civil libertarians and conservatives, limited the effects of the most stringent campaign finance reforms. The Court ruled that there can be no limits on a candidate's contributions to his or her own campaign, which may encourage even more wealthy people to involve themselves in

53. *Financing a Better Election System* (Committee for Economic Development, 1968).

politics directly. In the same decision the Court also said that a person could spend unlimited funds supporting a candidate if he or she did not coordinate the effort with the candidate's own campaign.[54]

Most important, perhaps, candidates with wealthy supporters can continue to use money in various "nonpolitical" ways to build name recognition and popularity. They can create task forces or fact-finding committees on highly visible or emotional issues, making it likely that their names will appear in the news. They can take "fact-finding" tours before they announce their candidacy. They can be hired as consultants or good-will representatives by businesses with nationwide operations. They can have a regular newspaper column or radio show as a political commentator.

Although the new law restricts individual donors to $1,000 gifts to each of 25 candidates for national-level offices, it permits these same individuals to give $5,000 per year to the political action committee of the corporation for which he or she works, and $20,000 a year to a committee of a national party. These committees, in turn, can give their accumulated funds to specific candidates—up to $5,000 per candidate in the case of the party committees. Not surprisingly, corporate-connected political action committees proliferated in the wake of the changes in the law—107 major corporations and 22 banks set up such committees in 1975 alone.[55]

Even the formula by which federal money is given to candidates in presidential primaries continues the advantage to those with wealthy backers. While other nations, such as Sweden, Norway and Germany, provide public financing on the basis of the number of people who give to the candidate, the American

54. Alexander, *Financing Politics, op. cit.*, pp. 149–151.
55. *Ibid.*, pp. 126–127.

law instead matches the amount of dollars contributed. Thus, Morris Udall had 3,000 more contributors than Carter in 1976, but received only half as much of the money provided by tax-payer checkoffs on income-tax returns ($1.9 million for Udall vs. $3.5 million for Carter) because his average donor did not con-tribute as much as Carter's wealthier backers. Fund raiser George E. Agree argues that this "means test" has a significant effect:

Money became more important than before, as success depended on having the resources to contest for delegates in each of thousands of precincts across the country. It is unlikely that Carter could have been so effective in taking advantage of the new rules without that extra $1,566,898 from the common pool of taxpayer dollars.[56]

Money, then, will remain a central element in determining who emerges victorious from the candidate-selection process. It is not the only element, as pluralists constantly remind us, but it is an essential one. The candidate who spends the most does not necessarily win, but the person who does not have a large war chest to begin with usually is eliminated quite early. It is the need for this large amount of start-up money—to develop name recognition, to gain legitimacy, to undertake direct-mail campaigns, to schedule radio and television advertising in ad-vance—that gives members of the power elite a very direct role in the process right from the start, permitting them direct access to politicians of both parties. Even if they do not tie specific strings to their money, as they often do not, the fund-raising process gives members of the power elite a chance to ensure that only people whom they consider sensible and approachable will emerge from party primaries.

56. George E. Agree, "How Reform Rigged the Election," the Washington *Post*, July 11, 1977, p. A–23.

THE EFFECTS OF ELECTORAL REFORM

Candidate selection through the two-party system has been by and large satisfactory to the American ruling class. Although the founding fathers did not consciously create the system, and indeed were opposed to the existence of political parties, the next generation of leaders came to understand the usefulness of a party system, and became its staunch defenders.[57] However, in the late nineteenth and early twentieth centuries the system began to produce results at the local level that were discomforting to leaders within the ruling class. Machine Democrats and even Socialists were electing more and more average people to city councils, threatening business control of city governments.

Members of the power elite became increasingly concerned about these electoral successes by the working class. In 1894 about 150 businesspeople, lawyers and academicians from 21 cities in 13 states met together in a National Conference for Good City Government. The conference led to the formation of a permanent National Municipal League three months later. Working through a special committee, the National Municipal League began to formulate a municipal program which would put into practice what the league saw as the essential principles that must underlie successful city government. The committee report, which became a model for charter revisions around the country, called for nonpartisan, city-wide elections, no salaries for council members and elections at times other than when state and national elections were being held.[58]

57. Richard Hofstadter, *The Idea of a Party System* (Univ. of California Press, 1969).

58. See Frank M. Stewart, *A Half Century of Municipal Reform: The History of the National Municipal League* (Univ. of California Press, 1950), for the origins and early program of the National Municipal League.

The general line of attack used by the ruling-class leaders was to criticize city government officials in the name of "reform." They charged that city government had come under the control of incompetent and often corrupt people who were wasting the taxpayers' money and inhibiting the growth of the city. They suggested that government should be run by "experts" who knew what they were doing and were beyond corruption. They were for "good government," which became the rallying cry for their reforms.

The specific mechanisms to bring about "good government" were several. First, elections should be "nonpartisan" in nature. Although it was still thought sensible to be Republican or Democrat at the national level, such partisan identifications were said to be harmful at the local level, where the issues were more technical and in need of expert solution. Second, local elections should not be held at the time of state and national elections, for local issues were supposedly separate from state and national issues. Third, local elections should be city-wide rather than by districts. The good-government forces developed numerous arguments about the evils of representing a specific district, mostly along the line that district elections led to a council that did not look out for the general interests of the city. In making this argument, of course, they ignored the fact that the Congress and state legislatures are based upon the district principle. Fourth, the reformers argued that council members should receive no salary. This would reduce the temptation to self-service and corruption, and encourage public-spirited citizens to stand for election.

In addition to these reforms, the good-government leaders added another one in the years 1910–1915. They argued that the city should be managed by an appointed administrative expert whose function would be much like that of the chief executive officer of a large corporation. The council, like a board of directors, would set general policy, and the city manager, like the chief executive officer, would carry out policy in an efficient and professional manner. The new idea was called the council-manager form of government.[59]

The actual goal of these reforms was to reduce working-class influence on city government. By removing party labels from candidates, it would be harder for low-income voters to identify their Democratic and Socialist friends. By changing the date of the elections, it was hoped that the hold of parties on the local electorate would be lessened, and the notion would grow that local issues were separate from state and national issues. District elections were opposed because the unwanted council members were coming from specific districts, namely, working-class districts. Making the elections city-wide would help dilute the strength of working-class candidates. They would lack name recognition outside their districts, and they would lack the money to campaign city-wide. The elimination of salaries for council service would make it more difficult for working people to serve, while encouraging the affluent to take part in "public service." The council-manager form of government was a general device to depoliticize city government. It was part of a mystique of efficiency and expertise that brands the average person as incompetent to make political judgments.[60]

The package of reforms slowly developed and publicized by the good-government leaders within the power elite came together as a general program of the National Municipal League.

59. See Stewart, *op. cit.*, and Richard J. Stillman, *The Rise of the International City Managers' Association* (Univ. of New Mexico Press, 1974), for the origins of the council-manager system.

60. Samuel P. Hayes, "The Politics of Reform in Municipal Government in the Progressive Era," *Pacific Northwest Quarterly*, October, 1964, provides an excellent historical and political analysis of how reforms benefited the ruling class and excluded the working class.

Aided by other reform organizations and local Chambers of Commerce, the new campaign had several important successes in the years just before World War I. The effort picked up momentum during and shortly after the war, when a campaign of physical attacks and jailings contributed to the destruction of the Socialist Party.[61] By 1919, 130 cities had adopted the council-manager plan, and hundreds more were to follow in the next few years. By 1965, over half the cities between 25,000 and 250,000 in population were functioning under council-manager government. The figure was 40 percent for all cities with more than 5,000 citizens, and the plan was especially popular in the suburbs.[62] In the largest of cities, however, the good-government movement usually was defeated by Democratic Party organizations in its attempts to enact council-manager government, and it had to settle for lesser reforms and continued dealings with the political machines.

Despite specific losses, however, the reforms were successful in accomplishing the underlying aims of the campaign. Working people, whether Democrats or Socialists, disappeared from the halls of city government, to be replaced by local business-people.[63] With their voices muted in city politics, ordinary people of course voted less in local elections. They were then criticized by the social scientists and the mass media for their failure to be interested in politics. This is called blaming the victim, the standard outcome of all ruling-class reforms.[64]

61. See James Weinstein, *The Corporate Ideal in the Liberal State* (Beacon Press, 1968), for the success of the campaign and the decline of the Socialists.

62. Leonard E. Goodall, *The American Metropolis* (Merrill Pub. Co., 1968), pp. 60–61.

63. Hayes, *op. cit.*; Weinstein, *op. cit.*

64. William Ryan, *Blaming the Victim* (Random House, 1971).

THE RESULTS OF CANDIDATE SELECTION

What kinds of politicians emerge from America's individualistically oriented candidate-selection process, with its mixture of partisan and nonpartisan politics, and its great reliance on large contributors? The answer is available from several studies. Politicians are first of all people from the higher levels of the social ladder. Generally speaking, about 9 of every 10 politicians in state and national offices come from the top 15 percent of the occupational ladder.[65] When attention is focused exclusively on the national level, politicians come from an even more narrow band of the social structure. A study of the 92nd Congress by psychologist Richard Zweigenhalf found that 66 percent of senators and 74 percent of representatives came from the 10 percent of families with business or professional occupations, and that virtually all of the senators and representatives were themselves professional people or former business executives. Only 5 percent of the senators had been farmers or ranchers, none had been workers; 3 percent of the representatives had been farmers or ranchers, 3 percent had union backgrounds. Zweigenhaft's comparison of his findings with a study of the Senate in the mid-1950's and of the House in the early 1940's showed that there had been very little change over that time span, except for a decrease in the number of farmers and a slight increase in the number of professionals and business executives.[66]

Few twentieth-century Presidents have been from outside the very wealthiest circles. Theodore Roosevelt, William H. Taft,

65. Donald R. Matthews, *The Social Background of Political Decision-Makers* (Doubleday, 1954), p. 28; Suzanne Keller, *Beyond the Ruling Class* (Random House, 1963), p. 310ff.

66. Richard Zweigenhaft, "Who Represents America?" *The Insurgent Sociologist*, Spring, 1975.

Franklin D. Roosevelt and John F. Kennedy were from wealthy families. Herbert Hoover and Jimmy Carter made their own money outside of politics. Lyndon B. Johnson was a millionaire several times over through his wife's land dealings and his use of political leverage to obtain a lucrative television license in Austin. Even Richard M. Nixon was a wealthy man when he finally attained the presidency in 1968, having made considerable money as a corporate lawyer between 1963 and 1968, due to his ability to open political doors for corporate clients. Politics at the highest levels of American society is a rich man's game.[67]

The politicians produced by the candidate-selection process are, second, at least among those who wish to go beyond local and state politics, enormously ambitious and driven people who are constantly striving for bigger and better things for themselves. To understand the behavior of a politician, notes one political analyst, "it is more important to know what he wants to be than how he got to where he now is."[68] This great ambition, whether it be for wealth or higher office, makes politicians especially available to those who can help them rise. Those who can aid them in this regard are very often wealthy people with money to contribute and connections to other districts, states or regions where the striving candidate needs new friends. Thus, even the most liberal of politicians may develop a new circle of supporters as he or she moves from the local to the congressional to the presidential level, gradually becoming more and more involved with the leading figures within the power elite.

Third, the products of the candidate-selection process are

67. For a study which shows that 13 of the first 36 Presidents were part of an upper-class kinship network of about 250 people, see Michael P. Merlie and Edward T. Silva, "The First Family: Presidential Kinship and Its Theoretical Implications," *The Insurgent Sociologist*, Spring, 1975.

68. Joseph A. Schlesinger, *Ambition and Politics* (Rand McNally Co., 1966), p. 5.

people who are by and large without strong policy preferences. Only rarely do those who go into politics in the United States have very strong ideological concerns. The exceptions to this statement on either the liberal or ultraconservative side come to mind so quickly and are so well known precisely because they are so unusual. Democratic politicians are generally less liberal than their highly motivated and ideologically concerned party workers. Republican politicians are usually less conservative than their zealous and ultraright supporters. These facts often produce feelings of disappointment and betrayal in the hearts of strong left and right partisans, but they bring comfort to members of the ruling class.

Finally, with the exception of the local level, where small-time business men and women are much more likely to sit on city councils, the system produces a set of politicians who are mostly lawyers. In 1972, for example, 70 percent of the senators and 51 percent of the representatives were lawyers, but the situation is about the same for earlier times and in most state legislatures. Of 995 elected governors for all states between 1870 and 1950, 46 percent were practicing lawyers. Twenty-five of the 39 American Presidents have been lawyers.[69]

The large percentage of lawyers in the American political system is highly atypical when compared with other countries, where only 10–30 percent of legislators have a legal background. An insight into this overrepresentation is gained by comparing the United States with a deviant case at the other extreme, Denmark, where only 2 percent of legislators are lawyers. The class-based nature of Danish politics in the late nineteenth century and the fact that political careers are not pathways to judicial

69. Heinz Eulau and John D. Sprague, *Lawyers in Politics* (Bobbs-Merrill, 1964), pp. 11–12. For information on local-level politicians, see Kenneth Prewitt, *The Recruitment of Political Leaders* (Bobbs-Merrill, 1970), pp. 124 and 157.

appointments seem to discourage lawyer participation. The Danish case suggests that the classless nature of American politics, combined with the intimate involvement of political parties in the judicial system, creates a political climate for lawyer domination of the political system.[70]

Whatever the reasons for their involvement, lawyers are an occupational grouping that by training and career needs produce ideal go-betweens and compromisers. They are the supreme "pragmatists" in a nation where pragmatism is a central element in the reigning ideology of nonideology.[71] They are taught to be "hired guns," and they are proud to be good at their trade. They are dispassionate about "the issues." They have been socialized to be discreet, and can claim the cloak of "lawyer-client" privilege when questioned about their work for clients. While some of them see politics as a vocation, and indeed became lawyers because they knew the law to be the best avenue to elected office, others see politics only as an opportunity to advance their law careers.

In a study of legislators in Connecticut, several lawyers who had just been elected to the state government explained their motivations to the investigator very frankly. One said the legislature was a "golden opportunity" to make valuable acquaintances. Another said that he saw other legislators as "very good contacts." The lawyer-legislator who is called an "advertiser" by political scientist James D. Barber is a person eager to move onward and upward, either in private practice or the judicial system:

70. Morgens D. Pedersen, "Lawyers in Politics: The Danish Folketing and United States Legislatures," in Samuel C. Patterson and John C. Wahlke, *Comparative Legislative Behavior* (Wiley & Sons, 1972).

71. Albert P. Melone, "Rejection of the Lawyer-Dominance Proposition: Is the Evidence Compelling?" *Meetings of the Political Science Section of the Minnesota Academy of Sciences*, April 29–30, 1977.

But—that's law—a lawyer cannot advertise. The only way that he can have people know he is in existence is by going to this meeting, going to that meeting, joining that club, this club, becoming a member of the legislature—so that people know that there is such a person alive.[72]

Lawyer-legislators in a four-state study were equally direct:

It was not so much for the political aspect of it. I went into politics really for selfish reasons. I'd been practicing law for less than a year, and this is a very good way to become better known in the community.

I was out of law school and thought of it as a measure of advertising myself before the public. That was the prime motive.[73]

A few lawyers serving in state legislatures actually were chosen by their law firms to run for office because it would be good for business. For example:

While in law partnership, it was decided that I would be the first one in the firm to run for office. . . . I was then chosen by the senior partners in the firm as having the best chance.[74]

Many of these ambitious lawyer-legislators at the state and national level work for corporate clients while they are in office. A significant number are on retainers from major businesses, which ensures them a minimum income of many thousands of dollars a year whether they do any work for the corporation or not. Many obtained their corporate clients after attaining

72. James D. Barber, *The Lawmakers* (Yale Univ. Press, 1965), pp. 68–69. Lawyers can now advertise, but it is likely that being a legislator will continue to be considered one of the best ways of becoming known.

73. Eulau and Sprague, *op. cit.*, p. 44.

74. *Ibid.* The ellipses are in the original.

office.[75] The relationship between their business interests and congressional vote is often very direct. When former Representative William Miller of New York, who ran as Barry Goldwater's vice presidential candidate in 1964, voted to reduce the tariff on the raw materials from which felt is made, he was receiving a $7,500 retainer from Lockport Felt Company. His law firm also represented Lockport Felt before the Federal Trade Commission in an antitrust case.[76]

As the foregoing makes clear, the major results of the candidate-selection process are, first, a large number of well-to-do politicians who are eager and willing to "go along to get along," precisely the kind of politicians who are necessary if the special-interest process is to operate the way it does, and second, a great many politicians with few strong policy positions of their own, who are thus open to the suggestions put forth to them by the corporate executives and academic experts who have been legitimated as "serious" statesmen and leaders within the institutions of the policy-planning process. In other words, the evidence shows that the candidate-selection process naturally produces the kinds of elected officials whom we knew must be in office because of the ways in which the special-interest and policy-planning processes operate. We can begin to see why the three processes mesh together so well even though they are relatively independent.

POLITICIANS AND THE POLICY PROCESS

Given the large number of pliable politicians produced by the electoral system, it is not unexpected that experts from the

75. Drew Pearson and Jack Anderson, *The Case Against Congress* (Simon and Schuster, 1968), chapter 4.
76. *Ibid.*, p. 204.

policy-planning network provide advice to both Republican and Democratic winners. This is especially the case at the crucial presidential level. As columnist Joseph Kraft wrote about the Council on Foreign Relations, "the Council plays a special part in helping to bridge the gap between the two parties, according unofficially a measure of continuity when the guard changes in Washington."[77] Nor is it surprising that Hubert Humphrey would reveal in early 1973 that he had asked Henry Kissinger before the 1968 election to serve as his foreign policy advisor should he win the presidency—meaning that whether Nixon or Humphrey won in 1968, one thing was sure: Henry Kissinger of the Council on Foreign Relations would be the primary foreign policy advisor.[78]

The general deference of politicians to the experts from the policy-planning establishment can be seen most clearly in the postelectoral behavior of John F. Kennedy and Jimmy Carter. After winning an election based on promises of a "new frontier" and charges of a nonexistent "missile gap," President-elect Kennedy called in Republican Robert Lovett, a Wall Street financier who was a friend of his father, and asked him for advice as to who should be appointed to important government positions. Lovett was, according to historian and Kennedy aide Arthur M. Schlesinger, Jr., the "chief agent" between Kennedy and an "American Establishment" of financiers and corporate lawyers who were an "arsenal of talent which had so long furnished a steady supply of always orthodox and often able people to Democratic as well as Republican administrations."[79] Lovett was indeed

77. Joseph Kraft, "School for Statesmen," *Harper's* magazine, July, 1958, p. 68.
78. "Humphrey and Kissinger," San Francisco *Chronicle*, March 12, 1973, p. 7.
79. Arthur M. Schlesinger, Jr., *A Thousand Days* (Houghton Mifflin, 1965), pp. 128–129.

an unusual advisor for a President-elect who had promised to get
the country moving again, but Kennedy now needed men to run
the government:

He had spent the last five years, he said ruefully, running for office,
and he did not know any real public officials, people to run a government, serious men. The only ones he knew, he admitted, were politicians, and if this seemed a denigration of his own kind, it was not
altogether displeasing to the older man. Politicians *did* need men to
serve, to run the government. The implication was obvious. Politicians
could run Pennsylvania and Ohio, and if they could not run Chicago,
they could at least deliver it. But could politicians run the world?
What did they know about the Germans, the French, the Chinese?
He needed experts for that, and now he was summoning them.[80]

Kennedy first asked Lovett if he would be interested in
serving as the Secretary of State, Defense or Treasury, but he
gracefully declined. When talk then turned to possible people
for those positions, Lovett named several. Among them were
Dean Rusk of the Rockefeller Foundation and the Council on
Foreign Relations, Robert McNamara of Ford Motor Company and C. Douglas Dillon of the investment firm Dillon, Read
and the Council on Foreign Relations. Kennedy solicited names
from other people, and there was intense lobbying for some of the
candidates, but in the end there was general consensus around
Rusk for Secretary of State, McNamara for Secretary of Defense
and Dillon for Secretary of the Treasury. Thus were three of the
most important policy positions in the new administration staffed.

The contrast between Carter's campaign rhetoric and his
deference to the established experts is equally great. As has been
discussed earlier in this chapter, one of Carter's main themes
was that he was not part of the mess in Washington. He was a

80. David Halberstam, *The Best and the Brightest* (Random House, 1972),
p. 4.

man of the people who would bring new faces into his administration. One of his top aides, Hamilton Jordon, went so far as to promise that two of the old faces—Cyrus Vance and Zbigniew Brzezinski—would never serve in a Carter administration: "If, after the inauguration, you find a Cy Vance as Secretary of State and Zbigniew Brzezinski as head of National Security, then I would say we failed. . . . The government is going to be run by people you never heard of." Indeed, Jordon would quit if Carter made such establishment appointments. Or so he told *Playboy* readers.[81]

Two of Carter's first appointments were Cyrus Vance and Zbigniew Brzezinski of the Council on Foreign Relations—the first as Secretary of State, the second as White House foreign policy advisor. (Jordon remained on as a White House aide to Carter.) Carter had come to know Vance and Brzezinski in the preceding three years as fellow participants in the Trilateral Commission, an international policy discussion group made up of American, West European and Japanese business leaders, politicians and intellectuals. It had been founded by the directors of the Council on Foreign Relations in 1972 to think about a "new world order." There soon followed the news that many Trilateral members—thirteen in all—were to become members of the new populist administration. They included the Secretary of Defense and the Secretary of the Treasury. The Carter administration was another sweep for the establishment, and Washington analysts fell all over themselves trying to figure out if the cabinet was more tied to the CFR, Brookings Institution, Rockefeller Foundation, IBM, Trilateral Commission, Coca-Cola or Wall Street.[82]

81. Robert Scheer, "Jimmy, We Hardly Know Y'All," *Playboy*, November, 1976, p. 192.

82. E.g., W. E. Barnes, "Carter Had Link to Insiders All Along," San Francisco *Examiner*, December 12, 1976, p. 1; "Carter's Brain Trusts," *Time*, December 20, 1976, p. 19; William Greider, "Trilateralists to Abound in

CONCLUSION

For all the talk about discussing the issues, politics in America has little to do with public policy. It provides little control of power-elite programs by the general populace. It is primarily a costly exercise in image-building, name-calling and gossip, and it serves as a kind of society-wide carnival and psychological safety valve. Conflict abounds within the process, but the policy-oriented concerns which motivate many of the party activists—and more of the general electorate than most social scientists realize—tend to get lost amidst the personal conflicts between ambitious candidates who are often seeking the rewards and excitement of higher office for their own personal gain and ego satisfaction.

The pluralist notion that public policy is influenced to any significant extent by the will of the majority through the competition between the two political parties is largely misguided. "Politics" is mostly for selecting ambitious, relatively issueless, upwardly mobile lawyers who have learned how to advance themselves by finding the rhetoric and rationalizations to implement both the narrow and general policies of the bipartisan power elite. "Ironically enough," concludes a skeptical political scientist, Michael Parenti, "the one institutional arrangement that is ostensibly designed to register the will of the many serves to legitimize the rule of the privileged few."[83]

There is more to American politics than fat cats and their political friends. There are serious-minded liberals who fight the good fight on many issues, ecologically oriented politicians who

Carter's White House," the Washington *Post*, January 16, 1977, p. 1; William Safire, "Carter's IBM Cabinet," the *New York Times*, January 17, 1977, p. 25.

83. Michael Parenti, *Democracy for the Few*, 2nd ed. (St. Martin's Press, 1977), p. 215.

remain true to their cause, and honest people of every political stripe who are not beholden to any wealthy people. But there are not enough of them, and they are often worn down by the constant pressure from lobbyists, lawyers and conventional politicians. As Representative Abner Mikva (D.-Ill.) once said, the system has a way of grinding you down:

The biggest single disappointment to a new man is the intransigence of the system. You talk to people and they say, "You're absolutely right, something ought to be done about this." And yet, somehow, we go right on ducking the hard issues. We slide off the necessary confrontations. This place has a way of grinding you down.[84]

It is also true that there are differences between Republicans and Democrats on certain issues. In particular, voting patterns reveal the greater willingness of Democrats to spend money on pork-barrel projects, economic pump-priming, agricultural assistance and social welfare.[85] In part this difference reflects the special needs of the Southern Democrats for federal assistance, but it also suggests that voting for Democrats sometimes has some payoff to those of average incomes and below.

However, even after acknowledging these differences, the fact remains that the friends and representatives of the working-class majority have not been able to win other than headlines, delays and an occasional battle. Despite the considerable efforts of organized labor and middle-income reformers, the candidate-selection process produces a predominance of politicians who sooner or later become sympathetic to the prevailing wisdom within either the moderate or ultraconservative faction of the power elite.

84. Robert Sherrill, "92nd Congress: Eulogies and Evasions," *The Nation*, February 15, 1971, p. 200.
85. Aage R. Clausen, *How Congressmen Decide* (St. Martin's Press, 1973).

5

The Ideology Process

The ideology process consists of the numerous methods through which members of the power elite attempt to shape the beliefs, attitudes and opinions of the underlying population. It is within this process that the power elite tries to create, disseminate and reinforce a set of attitudes and values that assure Americans that the United States is, for all its alleged defects, the best of all possible worlds. The ideology process is an adjunct to the other three processes, for they would not be able to function smoothly without at least the resigned acquiescence of a great majority of the population. Free and open discussion are claimed to be the hallmarks of the process, but past experience shows that its leaders will utilize deceit and violence in order to combat individuals or organizations which espouse attitudes and opinions that threaten the power and privileges of the ruling class.

The ideology process is necessary because public opinion does not naturally and automatically agree with the opinions of the power elite. The experiences of ordinary people on the job and in their daily lives often lead them to harbor private attitudes and to formulate personal opinions very different from those necessary for the ready acceptance of policies favored by the power elite. If such attitudes and opinions were to be publicly discussed and developed into alternative policies and new political strategies, the functioning of the special-interest, policy-planning and candidate-selection processes might be impaired, thereby threatening the economic relationships and governmental supports upon which the ruling class is based. Without the ideology process, a vague and amorphous public opinion—which often must be cajoled into accepting power-elite policies—might turn into a hardened class consciousness that opposed the ruling-class viewpoint at every turn.

In order to prevent the development of attitudes and opinions contrary to the interests of the ruling class, leaders within the ideology process attempt to build upon and reinforce the underlying principles of the American system. Academically speaking, these underlying principles are called laissez-faire liberalism, and they have enjoyed a near-monopoly of American political thought since at least the beginnings of the republic. The principles emphasize individualism, free enterprise, competition, equality of opportunity and a minimum of reliance upon government in carrying out the affairs of society. Their roots in the thinking of the greatest liberal philosophers of the seventeenth and eighteenth centuries—Locke, Hume, Montesquieu and Scottish Enlightenment thinkers—are long since lost from sight. Articulated for Americans by the founding fathers as part of the nation's revolutionary struggle with England, these values are enshrined in the basic documents of the nation, the Declaration of Independence and the Constitution.[1]

1. Louis Hartz, *The Liberal Tradition in America* (Harcourt, 1955); Francis X. Sutton et al., *The American Business Creed* (Harvard Univ. Press, 1956); Seymour M. Lipset, *The First New Nation* (Basic Books, 1963).

Popularly speaking, the values of laissez-faire liberalism are known to most citizens of the United States as "good Americanism." "Americanism"—including the all-important component of nationalism—is the world view or ideology of the United States. It is the complex set of rationales and rationalizations through which Americans interpret the world and justify their role within it. If they can be convinced that some policy or action is somehow part of this emotion-laden body of beliefs, they are likely to support it. Because everything must be done in the name of Americanism, the organizations that make up the ideology network strive to become the arbiters of which attitudes and opinions are good Americanism, and which are "un-American." They struggle to define for everyone what policies are in the "national interest" and to identify those policies with Americanism.

Not every issue is explicitly argued under the labels "American" and "un-American." Sometimes the argument is shaped in terms of specific aspects of Americanism. To be "practical," for example, is thought to be typically American. Thus, any idea that is not liked by leaders within the ideology process is branded as "theoretical" or "utopian," i.e., "un-American." An unacceptable idea also may be labeled as "foreign," which implies that it is derived from one or another "European philosopher," who are believed to be "impractical" and "utopian" thinkers.

One of the most important goals of the ideology network is to influence public schools, churches and voluntary associations set up by blue- and white-collar workers. To that end, organizations within the network have developed numerous links to these institutions. However, the middle-level organizations themselves are not part of the ideology network. Rather, they are relatively autonomous arenas within which the power elite must constantly contend with spokespersons of other social strata and political critics of the economic system. To assume otherwise would be to overlook the considerable conflict which takes place in many of these institutions and to deny any independence to other social strata.

Operating at the center of the ideology process are the same corporations, foundations and policy-planning groups that are part of the policy-formation process. In the case of the ideology network, however, these organizations link not only to government—as in the policy process—but to a large dissemination network which includes middle-class discussion groups, advertising agencies, public relations firms, corporate-financed advertising councils, special committees created to influence single issues and parts of the mass media. With the exception of the efforts through the mass media, which are intended to influence everyone, most of the organizations within the ideology network focus their attention on what are called the "attentive public." The attentive public are those people with college degrees and professional occupations who, due to their status and visibility, can be critical in shaping the opinions of the general public.

The way in which the policy process and the ideology process differ, even though the same organizations are at the center of both, is shown clearly in the work of the War and Peace study groups of the Council on Foreign Relations. Although those groups concentrated on formulating a set of policies to integrate a postwar international economy dominated by the United States, they also concerned themselves with the problem of how to generate public support for these programs. As one of the groups wrote in July, 1941, the "formulation of a statement of war aims for propaganda purposes is very different from formulation of one defining the true national interest."[2] The same group prepared the following statement for government officials:

2. Laurence H. Shoup and William Minter, *Imperial Brain Trust* (Monthly Review Press, 1977), p. 162.

If war aims are stated which seem to be concerned solely with Anglo-American imperialism, they will offer little to people in the rest of the world, and will be vulnerable to Nazi counterpromises. Such aims would also strengthen the most reactionary elements in the United States and the British Empire. The interests of other peoples should be stressed, not only those of Europe, but also of Asia, Africa, and Latin America. This would have a better propaganda effect.[3]

Based on this concern, leaders within the council made suggestions about what should be contained in a document stating United States war aims. The statement which ultimately issued from the government was the Atlantic Charter of August, 1941. President Roosevelt's chief advisor on the document was a council member who was close to the War and Peace project, Under-Secretary of State Sumner Welles. The charter spoke in terms of freedom, equality, prosperity and peace, but was very vague about American economic interests. The contrast between the economic and political aims which council leaders saw as "the true national interest" and the lofty generalities of the Atlantic Charter nicely define the difference between the policy and ideology processes. It also makes clear why two different networks are necessary for carrying the often-conflicting messages.

The ideology network is too big to describe completely. There are organizations which do public relations and education in virtually every issue area, in addition to organizations that do more general work. At its point of direct contact with the general public, the ideology network is extremely diverse and diffuse. The following sections can provide only selected examples from parts of this wide-ranging network.

3. *Ibid.*, pp. 162–163.

SHAPING OPINION ON
FOREIGN AFFAIRS

The way in which the ideology network functions is most readily apparent in the all-important area of foreign affairs. At the center of the network is the major policy-discussion group for foreign policy, the Council on Foreign Relations. The council itself does very little to influence public opinion directly. It publishes *Foreign Affairs*, the most prestigious journal in the field, and books which come out of its discussion groups. However, these publications make no attempt to reach the general public. They are primarily for consumption within the foreign-policy establishment.

For local elites, the council sponsors Committees on Foreign Relations in over thirty cities around the country. These committees meet about once a month to hear speakers provided by the council or the government. The aim of this program is to provide local leaders with information and legitimacy in the area of foreign affairs so they may function as opinion leaders on foreign-policy issues. As a 1951 council report explained:

In speaking of public enlightenment, it is well to bear in mind that the Council has chosen as its function the enlightenment of the leaders of opinion. These, in turn, each in his own sphere, spread the knowledge gained here [Committees on Foreign Relations] in ever-widening circles.[4]

The Committees on Foreign Relations were formed in the late 1930's with the aid of a grant from the Carnegie Corporation. According to the council member who had the major responsibility for organizing them, they quickly made their mark by playing "a unique role in preparing the nation for a bi-

4. *Ibid.*, p. 31.

partisan foreign policy in the fateful years that lay ahead."[5] Since that time they also have been involved in shaping public opinion on such crucial policy issues as the Marshall Plan and the recognition of the People's Republic of China.

The most important organization involved in shaping public opinion on foreign affairs is the Foreign Policy Association. It has an intensive program of literature and discussion groups to reach the "attentive public" of upper-middle-class professionals, academics and students. It sponsors a Great Decisions program and publishes the Headline Series pamphlets. It compiles foreign policy briefings that are sent to all incumbents and candidates for Congress. It attempts to get its material on radio programs and into extension courses, and it works closely with local World Affairs Councils to provide speakers and written material. The Foreign Policy Association is closely linked with the Council on Foreign Relations. According to Shoup and Minter, 42 percent of its directors for 1972 were members of the council.[6] Leaders within the power elite understand the complementary relationship of the two organizations. A council director of the 1930's wrote that the FPA had "breadth of influence," while the CFR had "depth." He saw the FPA as providing one of the "channel-ways of expression" that was necessary to attain "the support of the electorate."[7] A former president of the council explained to Shoup and Minter that the Committees on Foreign Relations attempted to reach top-level leaders, whereas the Foreign Policy Association attracted the "League of Women Voters type."[8]

The council and the association, in turn, are linked to other opinion-molding organizations influential in foreign affairs. One

5. *Ibid.*, p. 30.
6. *Ibid.*, p. 72.
7. *Ibid.*, p. 71.
8. *Ibid.*, p. 31.

is the American Assembly, which sponsors discussion groups around the country on a variety of issues. Another is the United Nations Association. There also are foreign affairs institutes at major universities which provide books and speakers that reflect the perspectives of the power elite on foreign policy.

The established organizations are supplemented when the need arises by special committees which focus on specific issues. One of the biggest efforts along this line was the Committee for the Marshall Plan, formed in 1947 to combat isolationists on the right wing. Chairing the committee was lawyer Henry L. Stimson, a former Secretary of War and Secretary of State who had been a council member since the 1920's. Five of the seven-member executive committee of the committee were affiliated with the council; the other two were labor leaders. The committee included as members 300 "prominent citizens" from every part of the country. Working with $150,000 in private contributions, it ran an all-out promotional campaign:

Regional Committees were promptly organized, the cooperation of scores of national organizations enlisted, and relevant publications given wide circulation. The committee promoted broad news and editorial coverage in metropolitan newspapers, set up a speakers' bureau, and employed a news agency which arranged for press releases, a special mat service for small town and country newspapers, and national and local radio broadcasts.[9]

In addition to its media barrage, the committee circulated petitions in every congressional district, and then sent the results to the individual representatives. It also had an office in Washington to keep in contact with Congress and to help prepare supportive testimony for appearances before legislative committees.

9. Harry B. Price, *The Marshall Plan and Its Meaning* (Cornell Univ. Press, 1955), p. 56.

The foreign-policy branch of the ideology network plays its most crucial role through its close involvement with the Executive branch of the federal government. Several studies of public opinion in the area of foreign policy suggest that the President and other foreign-policy decision-makers are the greatest influence on this type of opinion.[10] Political analyst Samuel Lubell provided a clear example of the President's central role in this area by means of interviews with a wide range of people shortly after the Russian Sputnik was launched in the late 1950's:

. . . especially striking was how closely the public's reactions corresponded to the explanatory "line" which was coming from the White House. . . . In talking about Sputnik, most people tended to paraphrase what Eisenhower himself had said. . . . In no community did I find any tendency on the part of the public to look for leadership to anyone else—to their newspapers, or radio commentators, to Congressmen, or to men of science. Nor, with some exception, could people be said to be in advance of the President, or to be demanding more action than he was.[11]

On foreign policy, the ideology network has been quite successful in shaping public opinion. Working through the White House, the State Department and the Department of Defense, and controlling most of the sources of information, the power elite has very few challenges on this issue. Political scientist James N. Rosenau concludes that the overwhelming majority of people are seldom aware of foreign-policy issues, read little about them and get what information they have from the mass

10. E.g., James N. Rosenau, *Public Opinion and Foreign Policy* (Random House, 1961), p. 63.; Samuel P. Huntington, *The Common Defense* (Columbia Univ. Press, 1961), pp. 235, 238 and 239.

11. Samuel Lubell, "Sputnik and American Public Opinion," *Columbia Univ. Forum*, Winter, 1957, p. 18.

media.[12] Another political scientist, Samuel P. Huntington, comes
to similar conclusions from case studies of military and defense
policies. He finds the public-opinion poll evidence against any
determinative influence by public opinion so "overwhelming"
that "even a wide margin of error would not invalidate the
conclusions drawn from them."[13]

The one foreign-policy issue where public opinion may appear
to have become independent from the President and other opinion leaders was the war in Vietnam. Even here, however, changes
in foreign policy and the opinions of political leaders seem to
have had a greater effect on public opinion than public opinion
had on foreign policy. For example, until the bombing of Hanoi
and Haiphong began in late spring 1966, the public was split
50–50 on the question of bombing. When asked in July, 1966,
after the bombing began, if "the administration is more right
or more wrong in bombing Hanoi and Haiphong," 85 percent
favored the bombing, while only 15 percent opposed it.[14] Conversely, a majority (51 percent) opposed a bombing halt in
March, 1968, but when asked one month later if they approved
or disapproved of a decision President Johnson had made in the
interim to stop the bombing of North Vietnam, only 26 percent
disagreed with the President. Sixty-four percent agreed with the
President and 10 percent had no opinion.[15] College-educated
adults and people of younger age groups were most likely to
show this "follower effect," that is, a change in opinion shortly
after a presidential initiative. Thus, it seems unlikely that public
opinion had any great influence on American decisions concerning Vietnam. Despite the strong protests against the war by col-

12. Rosenau, *op. cit.*

13. Huntington, *op. cit.*, pp. 238–239.

14. John E. Mueller, *War, Presidents and Public Opinion* (Wiley & Sons,
1973), p. 70, Table 4.2.

15. *Ibid.*, pp. 72 ff., Table 4.3.

lege students on large university campuses, public opinion in general tended to follow the initiatives of the President and the opinions of other decision-makers and party leaders.[16]

American foreign policy is not conducted without conflict and constraint. Most of this conflict, however, is due to the actions of other nations and to disagreements between moderates and ultraconservatives within the power elite. Because it builds on the deep-seated feelings of nationalism and patriotism that are the *sine qua non* of a modern nation, the ideology network has been able to function quite successfully in the critical area of foreign policy.

EDUCATION IN ECONOMICS

Shaping public attitudes on domestic issues is more difficult than on foreign policy, especially when there is no threat of a menacing external enemy to bind people together in common sacrifice. People have their own experiences to build on in thinking about domestic issues, and they see domestic issues as directly affecting their day-to-day lives.

One of the most important domestic issues concerns the functioning of the economy. Because most people are blue- and

16. See *Ibid.*, chapter 5, for a summary of poll evidence and references to earlier studies. Although public *opinion* probably had very little influence on policy, the *disruptions* caused by uprisings in the ghettos and by antiwar marches and other activities of students did play a role in ending the war. The militant actions of these two segments of the population—segments which were far less than a majority of the population—were of major concern to foreign policy advisors. Nonetheless, it was primarily the Viet Cong's Tet offensive that convinced American leaders they would have to draw back, and they did so believing the general situation in Southeast Asia had changed in their favor since the early 1960's due to the Sino-Soviet split and the destruction of the Indonesian Communist Party.

white-collar workers who want better salaries and less inflation, they are often critical of corporations. Many of them see corporations as operating to produce large profits for the few, and caring little about the ordinary person.

This attitude is vexing to corporate leaders. They believe it is due to "economic illiteracy," and they argue that it would change if people had the facts about the functioning of the corporations and the economy. They have spent tens of millions of dollars trying to present the facts as they see them. An analysis of how the power elite attempts to shape economic attitudes is a case study in how the ideology network reaches into the school system on an issue of concern to it.

The major organization in the field of economic education for the past thirty years has been the Joint Council on Economic Education. It was founded in 1949 because leaders within the Committee for Economic Development felt that there was a need for better education in economics. In its early years the joint council was formally affiliated with the CED, and received much of its funding from the Ford Foundation. Since 1964 it has been an independent organization, although its business-dominated board of directors has many common members with the CED.[17] Most of its financial support now comes from corporations and corporate foundations. Its biggest donors in 1975 were the American Bankers Association, AT&T, International Paper Company Foundation, the J.M. Foundation, Northern Natural Gas Company, the Sears, Roebuck Foundation, the Sloan Foundation and the Department of Health, Education and Welfare.

The focus of the joint council is on the education system. It attempts to educate teachers in the teaching of economics. It publishes books, pamphlets and teaching aids. It provides school

---

17. Karl Schriftgiesser, *Business and Public Policy* (Prentice-Hall, 1967), chapter 22. The chapter is entitled "Fighting Economic Illiteracy."

systems with curriculum guides. Most importantly, perhaps, it attempts to shape college programs in teacher training. The joint council began its efforts in the late 1940's and early 1950's with in-service mini-courses and summer workshops to train teachers in economics. That program has expanded to the point where in 1974 17,000 teachers participated in the in-service workshops and 2,500 took part in 84 summer workshops.[18]

Graduates of the early workshops provided the joint council with the basis for local and regional councils on economic education. These affiliated but autonomous councils are designed to provide support for economic education in the schools. By 1958 thirteen of the affiliated councils were operating with full-time field directors.[19] Only Alaska, Michigan and Vermont lacked affiliated councils by 1975.

Although the development of textbooks and curricula were part of the joint council's programs in the 1950's, it did not get into this area in a big way until 1964 when it launched a $2.5-million experimental program in several school districts to test teaching methods and new written materials. The program was designed to introduce some aspects of economics as early as the first grade.[20] This project continued into the 1970's as the Cooperating Schools Program, involving 235 schools in curriculum improvement in the teaching of economics.

Just as important as improving curricula in the joint council's overall strategy is its program to include the teaching of economics as one part of the teacher-training credential at colleges

18. Joint Council on Economic Education, *Annual Report*, 1975, p. 3.

19. M. L. Frankel, "The Joint Council on Economic Education: The First Ten Years," *National Association of Secondary School Principals*, October, 1958, p. 124.

20. "Upgrading Economics," *Scholastic Teacher*, November 11, 1964, p. 1; "Economics Council Expands School Program," *Business Education World*, September, 1964, p. 4.

and universities. This program has its strongest basis in the 122 council-affiliated Centers for Economic Education at colleges and universities in forty-eight states. The joint council considers it a major gain that the percentage of teacher-training programs requiring social-studies teachers to take an economics course has risen from 50 percent in 1967 to 73 percent in 1975. The percentage for elementary teachers has risen even more dramatically, from 13 percent to 32 percent.[21]

The program of the joint council, then, begins in corporate board rooms and foundation offices, flows through affiliated councils and university centers, and ends up in teacher-training programs and public school curricula. The joint council lists the Business Roundtable, the National Association of Manufacturers, the American Petroleum Institute, the American Farm Bureau and the AFL-CIO among its cooperating organizations. It has an affiliate relationship with eleven different associations of education officials. And yet, according to polls, the level of economic illiteracy remains as high as ever in the adult population.

The continuing high level of economic illiteracy generates concern and renewed efforts by leaders within the ideology network. It spawns new organizations to profit from it by selling seminars, films and teaching aids.[22] On the other hand, not all is gloom for the corporate community. Despite the illiteracy— and criticisms of specific corporations and their practices—there is still the fact that most people state a belief in free enterprise and profits:

Our work shows that better than nine out of ten will certainly take strong exception to any threat to free enterprise. Even as many as

21. Joint Council on Economic Education, *Annual Report*, 1975, p. 3.
22. "Americans are Economically 'Illiterate,'" San Francisco *Chronicle*, November 26, 1977, p. 44.

three out of four feel that the role of profits is very clear—it's for the good of the country—and some even reinforce their belief in profits, or the profit motive, in terms of calling it a moral thing. It's moral to have a profit system because then, truly, the deserving get rewarded.[23]

ADVERTISING IN THE PUBLIC INTEREST

Advertising is everywhere in the United States. There is no escaping it. Most of it goes in one ear and out the other—or so we think. Advertising, as we know, is used by corporations primarily to sell specific products. But it can be used to sell the system as well.

Many corporations attempt to sell the free-enterprise system through what is called institutional advertising. Instead of talking about their product, they tell what they have done to benefit local communities, schools or service organizations. Other corporations promote a good image of themselves by sponsoring programs on public television, providing funds for local charities, or donating services to community organizations.

The most pervasive and systematic use of advertising by the ideology network can be seen in the functioning of the Advertising Council. Formed during World War II to help the war effort, it is a big-business organization which has done billions of dollars of public-interest advertising in its thirty-five years of existence. The council's war effort was judged so successful in promoting the image of corporate business that it was continued in the postwar period as an agency to support Red Cross, United Fund, conservation, population control, urban renewal, religion in American life and other campaigns which its corporate-dominated boards and advisory committees determine to be in

23. Florence R. Skelly, "The Changing Attitudes of Public Opinion," *Public Relations Journal*, November, 1976, pp. 15–16.

the public interest.[24] Perhaps its best-known figure in the past was Smokey the Bear.

The Advertising Council, with an annual budget of only $2 million, each year places about $460 million worth of free advertising on radio and television, in magazines and newspapers, and on billboards and public buses. After the council leaders decide on which campaigns to endorse, the specifics of the program are given to one or another Madison Avenue advertising agency which does the work without charge.

Most council campaigns seem relatively innocuous and in a public interest that nobody would dispute. However, as Glenn K. Hirsch's detailed study of these campaigns shows, even these programs have an ideological slant. For example, the council's ecology ads do not point the finger at corporations or automobiles as the prime cause of a dirty environment. They suggest instead that "People start pollution, people can stop it," thereby putting the responsibility on individuals. A special subcommittee of the council's Industry Advisory Committee gave very explicit instructions as to how this ad campaign should be formulated. It wrote: "The committee emphasized that the [advertisements] should stress that each of us must be made to recognize that each of us contributes to pollution, and therefore everyone bears the responsibility."[25] Thus, the campaign was geared to deflect growing criticism of the corporate role in pollution, as well as to show corporate concern about the environment. Similarly, the council's Traffic Safety Campaign emphasizes drunk drivers rather than poorly designed and unsafe vehicles as the major problem in causing accidents.[26]

24. Glenn K. Hirsch, "Only You Can Prevent Ideological Hegemony: The Advertising Council and Its Place in the American Power Structure," *The Insurgent Sociologist*, Spring, 1975.

25. *Ibid.*, p. 69.

26. *Ibid.*, p. 67.

Along with its standard support of voluntary organizations, the council tries to create a receptive climate for new government programs. In the mid-1950's, for example, it ran a series of advertisements on urban renewal and urban redevelopment in conjunction with a corporate and government drive to get urban renewal programs into high gear.[27] In the early 1970's it ran ads downgrading the importance of a college education and praising technical training. This campaign came at a time when corporate and government officials foresaw a surplus of college graduates on the job market. The ads, featuring former Chicago Bears halfback Gale Sayers, urged listeners to write the Department of Health, Education and Welfare for a free booklet produced through a cooperative effort by the U.S. Office of Education, the Conference Board and the Manpower Institute.[28]

The council also tries to help restore order in times of crisis. Between 1965 and 1971, "expenditures by the media in support of council campaigns jumped by an unprecedented 96 percent."[29] Most of this effort was directed at ghetto unrest. One set of commercial messages in 1965 urged people to "Put Your Racial Problems on the Table—Keep Them off the Streets." In 1970 the council had over a hundred notables from business, labor, sports and politics demonstrate racial harmony by joining together to sing "Let the Sun Shine" from the hit musical *Hair.* In a more practical vein, the council ran a "Crisis Series" which urged businesspeople to give jobs to ghetto blacks. This series resulted in more pages of advertisements in the business press than had ever been given to a single campaign.[30] The council also adapted its Religion in American Life Series to the crisis situation. The

27. "Action on Slums," the *New York Times*, November 19, 1954, p. 39.
28. "25 Technical Careers You Can Learn in 2 Years or Less" (U.S. Office of Education, n.d.).
29. Hirsch, *op. cit.*, p. 77.
30. *Ibid.*, p. 76.

previous message had urged that people attend and support the church of their choice. By 1968 that series was suggesting that people remove violence from their lives and their communities.

Even when council campaigns attempt to influence current social problems, they are seldom controversial. This pattern was broken in 1976, however, by an attempt to aid in the battle for "economic understanding." Disturbed by some of the poll data suggesting considerable public hostility to corporations in the wake of Watergate, overseas bribes and the energy crisis, council leaders launched the largest campaign in the organization's history. Spending $2.5 million for production costs alone, the campaign was geared to take advantage of the nation's bicentennial celebration. Since it is impossible to teach economics in brief television ads or on billboards, the idea of the campaign was to induce people to send away for a booklet which easily and clearly explained the economic system.[31] Entitled "The American Economic System . . . and Your Part In It," the attractive twenty-page publication was illustrated with cartoons wherein Charlie Brown and other Peanuts characters discuss their problems in coping with economic questions.

The first problem for the campaign arose when liberals learned that part of its funding—$239,000—came from the Department of Commerce. Worse, the money came from programs earmarked to help minorities and the poor.[32] The next problem appeared when both liberals and ultraconservatives attacked the content of the booklet from their respective ideological positions. Liberals were annoyed that the booklet barely discussed poverty

31. "Council Shapes Huge Campaign," the *New York Times*, December 4, 1975, p. 71.

32. Michael J. Connor, "Ad Campaign That Seeks to Explain Workings of Free Enterprise System Stirs Controversy," *The Wall Street Journal*, August 4, 1976, p. 30.

and unemployment. Ultraconservatives were miffed that it was too friendly toward government intervention and a "mixed economy"; they felt that the virtues of unadulterated free enterprise should have been extolled more fully. The final embarrassment to the campaign came when CBS and ABC refused to run the first series of advertisements for fear that they would have to give equal time to Americans for a Working Economy, a coalition of progressives and economic democrats who had prepared a booklet calling for an economy that permitted greater consumer and worker participation in both the decision-making and rewards of the economic system.

Undaunted, the Ad Council moved ahead with its program. In July, 1977, it announced to its members that it had developed a new radio and television advertising theme around the concept of an "economic quotient." "How High is Your Economic Quotient?" asked the ads. If the listener could not answer certain questions, then he or she had a low "E.Q.," and should write for the free booklet.[33] The council also stepped up its efforts to distribute the booklet through the print media and schools. Several airlines were induced to include the booklet among the reading matter available in airplane seat pockets. The American Advertising Federation and its 165 local clubs endorsed the campaign and adopted it as their major activity for 1977. Junior Achievement, the National Association of Manufacturers, the Council of Better Business Bureaus and the General Federation of Women's Clubs urged their affiliates to sponsor the "economic understanding" campaign at the local level. By the end of 1977, 1½ million copies of the council's booklet had been distributed to public schools, civic groups and business groups. The adver-

33. "Advertising Council Reveals Plans to Launch E.Q. Quiz Campaign in Mid-September," *Economic Communicator* (Advertising Council, July, 1977).

tising message concerning the booklet had appeared on over 400 television stations, 1,000 radio stations, in 3,000 daily and weekly newspapers and on 110,000 buses, commuter trains and subways.[34]

Americans for a Working Economy, on the other hand, had very little success in placing its advertising messages with television stations. A letter to NBC asking for public-service time under the Federal Communications Commission "fairness doctrine" was rejected by the network because the group's ads were said to be obviously controversial.

The effectiveness of the Ad Council's programs is open to question. It is not clear that they have a direct influence on very many opinions. At the least, however, they create good will among the leaders of the middle-strata voluntary associations whose specific campaigns are promoted. Beyond that, the effects are not easy to gauge, for neither social scientists nor the advertising industry is able to assess accurately the influence of this kind of advertising. In general, studies suggest that advertising campaigns of a propagandist nature work best "when used to reinforce an already existing notion or to establish a logical or emotional connection between a new idea and a social norm."[35] But even when an ad campaign can be judged a failure in this limited role, it at least has filled a vacuum that might have been used by a competing group. This is especially the case in television. The Advertising Council utilizes 80 percent or more of the public-service advertising time that television networks must provide by law.[36] Thus, Hirsch concludes his assessment of the effectiveness of the council's advertising by stressing both its posi-

34. "Status Report on the Advertising Council's Public Service Campaign on the American Economic System," Advertising Council Report, n.d. The subtitle of this report is "The Most Successful Introduction of a Public Service Campaign in Advertising Council History."

35. Hirsch, op. cit., p. 78.

36. Ibid., p. 79.

tive and negative effects: "Its commercials reinforce and channel existing values, while simultaneously preventing groups with a different ideology from presenting their interpretation of events."[37]

In addition to its efforts to influence the general public, the council has two functions within the power elite itself. First, it holds forums and discussion groups to develop new ways of explaining the American system. During the 1950's the council sponsored nine "Roundtables on American Life" which brought together business leaders, university professors and journalists to discuss a variety of problems. The 1956 session led to the widespread campaign to portray the United States as a "people's capitalism" in which "a very large percentage of the workers own the means of production, and under which workers fully share in the advantages of our expanding output through higher wages and more abundant goods at lower prices."[38] The idea did not catch on within the United States, but was used widely overseas by the United States Information Agency. The 1959 Roundtable, held in conjunction with several professors at the University of Chicago, produced a booklet for journalists and public-relations officials—"Major Economic Groups and National Policy"—to use in explaining the positive role of lobbyists and interest groups in the United States. The council was reacting to the belief it thought to be held by many that pressure groups were part of a "sinister entity" that is the hidden government of the United States.[39] As the introduction to the booklet states:

Frequently, individuals have drawn the conclusion that policy making lies in the hands of a small and powerful class. This conclusion is a

37. *Ibid.*
38. *Ibid.*, p. 75.
39. "Pressure Groups Called Integral: Chicago Group Says Most Perform Governmental Function in the Open," the *New York Times*, July 12, 1958, p. 48.

gross misunderstanding of the political processes by which political and economic power is diffused and which extend the wide sharing of economic benefits in a people's capitalism.[40]

The council's think-tank activities are now conducted under the auspices of a Public Policy Committee. The committee devises panels on such topics as the environment or social problems and also brings in speakers who are concerned with the public image of the corporate community as a whole. In late 1971, for example, the council heard David Rockefeller begin by saying that American business was facing its most severe disfavor since the 1930's. Business stood accused of "deceiving the consumer, destroying the environment, and disillusioning the younger generation."[41] Rockefeller then suggested that businesspeople must become reformers rather than merely striking back at critics. His general message would not be lost on the numerous sailing enthusiasts within the power elite:

In dealing with critics, I think all businesses would do well to keep in mind the words of Justice Oliver Wendell Holmes, a master of judicial summation. "We must sail sometimes with the wind, sometimes against it," he said. "But we must sail and not drift or lie at anchor."[42]

A second function of the council within the power elite itself is to encourage the business community to develop the kind of "social responsibility" that is implied by a speech such as David Rockefeller's. To this end the council popularizes new corporate programs which it hopes other corporations will emulate. It also

40. *Major Economic Groups and National Policy* (American Roundtable Committee of the Advertising Council, 1958), p. 1.

41. David Rockefeller, "Role of Business in an Era of Growing Accountability," Los Angeles *Times*, January 3, 1972, Part II, p. 7.

42. *Ibid.*

gives an annual Public Service Award to those corporate leaders who have done the most to encourage a long-range view among fellow businesspeople. The awards dinner at which the recipients are honored is an occasion for exhortative speeches to the assembled elite. In 1970 the president of CBS spoke as follows:

1970 has not been an easy year for most of us, and for some, it has been an unusually difficult year. In such a year, the term "public service" takes on a more vital meaning, for it becomes all the more essential that business take a broad view of its mission and display a clear sense of its obligation to the national interest.[43]

The Advertising Council is in some ways unique because of its prominence, massive resources and wide-ranging concerns. In its major activities, however, it is typical of a wide variety of ideology organizations that function in specific areas from labor relations to the arts. Those functions are basically three in number:

1. It provides think-tank forums where academics, journalists and other cultural experts can brainstorm with corporate leaders about problems of ideology and public opinion.
2. It helps to create class consciousness within the ruling circles through forums, booklets, speeches and awards.
3. It disseminates its version of the national interest to the underlying population.

THE LATENT FUNCTIONS OF THE IDEOLOGY PROCESS

Despite the best efforts of public-relations experts, advertising agents, industrial psychologists, media consultants and numerous other cultural technicians, the tens of millions of dollars spent

43. Hirsch, *op. cit.*, p. 72.

each year by corporations, foundations and policy groups on the molding of public opinion have not been able to bring about hearty endorsement of all power-elite policies by a majority of the underlying population. After years of effort, for example, there is still "economic illiteracy" that sometimes manifests itself in hostility to the corporate order.

The inability of the ideology network to engineer whole-hearted consent reveals the limits on that process, limits that are imposed by the class situation of the general populace and the opposing opinions advocated by trade unionists, liberals, social-ists and ultraconservatives. However, the continuing ideological conflict within the nation does not mean that the ideology net-work has failed in its task. Although it has not been able to bring about active acceptance of all power-elite policies and perspec-tives, it has been able to ensure that opposing opinions have remained isolated, suspect and only partially developed. As one sociologist notes, "The hegemonic process does not create a value consensus but confusion, fragmentation, and inconsistency in belief systems."[44] Thus, the most important role of the ideology network may be in its ability to help ensure that an alternative view does not consolidate to replace the resigned acquiescence and disinterest that are found by pollsters and survey researchers to permeate the political and economic consciousness of Ameri-cans at the lower levels of the socioeconomic ladder.[45] What Hirsch noted in relation to the latent function of the Advertising Council is applicable to the ideology network as a whole:

In order to preserve ideological hegemony, it is only necessary for the ruling group to reinforce dominant values and at the same time *prevent*

44. David Sallach, "Class Domination and Ideological Hegemony," *The Sociological Quarterly*, Winter, 1974, p. 42.
45. Michael Mann, "The Social Cohesion of Liberal Democracy," *American Sociological Review*, June, 1970.

the dissemination of opinion that effectively challenges the basic assumptions of the society. Public knowledge of inequality and injustice isn't so damaging as long as these perceptions are not drawn together into a coherent, opposing ideology.[46]

But the effects of the ideology network also go to a deeper and more subtle level. Even though many people do not accept the overt messages in the ads, booklets and speeches emanating from the ideology network, they often unwittingly accept the covert message that their problems lie in their own personal inadequacies. Liberal ideology, with its strong emphasis on individuality and personal responsibility, not only rewards the successful, it blames the victims. As psychologist William Ryan has shown, even the most well-meaning of political liberals have contributed to the development of a set of system-serving rationalizations which downplay the role of social forces and social relations in explaining social problems in the United States. Educational failure, teen-age pregnancies, black unrest—and other phenomena which are best understood in terms of the way our class system operates—are turned into reproaches of the victims for their alleged failure to correct personal defects and take advantage of the opportunities provided them.[47]

The campaign against economic illiteracy is a good example of Ryan's general point. Although the campaign failed to eliminate negative opinions about corporate capitalism, it succeeded in presenting the problem as one of "illiteracy," a cardinal sin in a country where everyone supposedly has the opportunity to be literate if they will but avail themselves of it. The Advertising Council even offered a free booklet to correct this personal defect.

46. Hirsch, *op. cit.*, p. 79. Italics in the original. For a similar argument from a different theoretical perspective, see the excellent article by Peter M. Hall, "A Symbolic Interactionist Analysis of Politics," *Sociological Inquiry*, 3–4, 1972.

47. William Ryan, *Blaming the Victim* (Random House, 1971).

If you did not write away for this booklet, that is, if you *chose to remain an economic illiterate*, then you should be ashamed of yourself and remain silent in economic debates. That is the underlying message of the campaign against economic illiteracy.

Richard Sennett and Jonathan Cobb, through in-depth interviews with working people in Boston, have provided a sensitive social-psychological account of how liberal ideology leaves working people with a paralyzing self-blame for their personal "failures," even though they know the social system is not fair to them. Sennett and Cobb have captured the way in which liberal ideology both gives Americans the hope of individual fulfillment and entraps them psychologically within a confining class structure that makes it very difficult to realize that fulfillment or think about changing the social system:

Workingmen intellectually reject the idea that endless opportunity exists for the competent. And yet, the institutions of class force them to apply the idea to themselves: *If I don't escape being part of the woodwork, it's because I didn't develop my powers enough.* Thus, talk about how arbitrary a class society's reward system is will be greeted with general agreement—with the proviso that in my own case I should have made more of myself.[48]

Sennett and Cobb then suggest that this self-blame is intimately related to questions of social change. Self-blame is important in understanding the reluctant acquiescence of wage earners in an unjust system:

Once that proviso [that in my own case I should have made more of myself] is added, challenging class institutions becomes saddled with

48. Richard Sennett and Jonathan Cobb, *The Hidden Injuries of Class* (Random House, 1972), pp. 250–251. For an earlier insightful discussion which makes a similar point on the basis of interviews with fifteen workingmen in New Haven, see Robert Lane, *Political Ideology* (Free Press, 1962).

the agonizing question, Who am I to make the challenge? To speak of American workers as having been "bought off" by the system or adopting the same conservative values as middle-class suburban managers and professionals, is to miss all the complexity of their silence and to have no way of accounting for the intensity of pent-up feeling that pours out when workingpeople do challenge higher authority.[49]

The double message of liberal ideology is what gives more potency than meets the eye to the power-elite network which disseminates that ideology. Those who do not believe the overt messages they hear from it are nonetheless left with a feeling that they are somehow to blame for their doubts and frustrations. The power elite benefits either way—active acceptance of the system by middle-status people who attribute their relative success to their wonderful personal abilities, or resigned acquiescence by ordinary workingpeople who secretly think of themselves as failures. The result is the perpetuation of a social system, based in principle upon equality and democratic process, which rewards a few with great wealth while punishing the vast majority with a life of unnecessary insecurity and anxiety.

THE ENFORCEMENT OF IDEOLOGY

The pervasiveness of liberal ideology can be overstated. Not everyone in the nation has been reduced to resigned acquiescence or personal grumbling. There are people who speak out in a clear fashion against the failures of the social system and advocate solutions to the inequities they perceive. Such people are dealt with through the enforcement aspect of the ideology process,

49. *Ibid.*, p. 251.

thereby demonstrating to less vocal people that there are costs to active opposition.

The attempt to enforce an ideological consensus is carried out in a variety of ways that include pressure, intimidation and violence. Those who are outspoken in their challenge to one or another of the main tenets of the American ideology may be passed over for promotions or fired from their jobs. They may be excluded from social groups or criticized in the mass media. If they get too far outside the consensus, they are harassed and spied upon by government agencies, as in the case of Martin Luther King, Jr., and numerous antiwar activists. If they form political groups, these groups may be infiltrated and disrupted.

The repressive power of the ruling class may or may not be the "basic reality" of the state in capitalist society, as most Marxists assert. But even if they overstate their case, as is believed by those theorists who emphasize the patriotic and ideological basis of the state, the fact remains that leaders within the American ruling class have turned loose strikebreakers, the police, the FBI and the CIA on trade-union organizers, civil-rights activists, antiwar protesters and left-wing political leaders, sometimes murdering them in the process.[50] These actions are part of the ideology process, and they suggest that the power elite will use the most drastic of methods to defend its position.[51]

50. For a Marxist who criticizes the traditional Marxian emphasis on "coercion and repression" because these factors alone "could not possibly, in the case of many if not most of these regimes, explain why they endured," see Ralph Miliband, *Marxism and Politics* (Oxford Univ. Press, 1977), p. 43.

51. For a glimpse into the hostility with which corporate leaders view reform movements and the general electorate, and their widespread distrust of the democratic system, see Leonard Silk and David Vogel, *Ethics and Profits: The Crisis of Confidence in American Business* (Simon and Schuster, 1976).

THE IDEOLOGY PROCESS
IN PROPER PERSPECTIVE

The ideology process is not the sole basis for ruling-class domination of the United States. People would not suddenly resist or revolt if they were to lose faith in the liberal world view. As sociologist Michael Mann has argued, an overemphasis on ideology tends to make every person into a kind of contemplative philosopher motivated primarily by abstract beliefs. Such a view does not give proper weight to the fact that the "institutional fit" between the daily lives of citizens and the central institutions of the society helps give a social system its stability: "A stable society is, therefore, one whose central institutions interlock and involve the activities of its citizens."[52] Routine involvement in a daily round of social activities—and particularly in a job—is one of the most important factors in social control and social stability.

From this perspective, the ideology process should be seen as no more basic than the three processes outlined in earlier chapters. It is in the special-interest, policy-formation and candidate-selection processes that the decisions are made which affect the prosperity of the economy and the success or failure of foreign policy, and hence the stability of overall institutional arrangements. The ideology process can help to make the other three processes function more smoothly, and it can help to maintain loyalty in the face of some degree of economic and social dislocation, but it cannot compensate for large-scale failures in the other processes.

Even though the ideology process is often unable to prevent disorder in the face of breakdown in the economy or failure in war, it does play a role in how that disorder will be resolved. If

52. Michael Mann, "The Ideology of Intellectuals and Other People in the Development of Capitalism," in Leon N. Lindberg et al., eds., *Stress and Contradiction in Modern Capitalism* (Lexington Books, 1975), p. 277.

an alternative view of social arrangements has gained a following, then there is the possibility that the power elite will not be able to restore order on its own terms. It is in this kind of situation that a coalition between left-wing activists and the working class becomes a distinct possibility and a threat to the ruling class. Indeed, the potential for this type of coalition helps to explain the unending war the ideology network conducts against the small number of socialists in the United States. If socialist critics can be constantly discredited as irrational extremists in times of relative quietude, it is less likely that they will be able to find adherents for their viewpoint during periods of crisis. And as Mann stresses in criticizing the Marxist assumption that intellectuals help to justify the social system, most intellectuals have in fact been "subversive of the capitalist structure of the West." Once capitalism became dominant, Mann argues, it required technicians, not intellectuals.[53] One of the functions of those technicians in the United States is to battle socialist intellectuals through the ideology network.

In summary, the ideology network is not the be-all and end-all of ruling-class domination. It has a role to play in reinforcing underlying liberal values and combating intellectual and political critics of the system, but it must be seen as functioning in the context of the other three processes and the overall success of the economic system. It does not function to eliminate conflict, but to keep conflict from leading to an alternative ideology that provides the basis for an anticorporate, anticapitalist social movement.

CONCLUSION

The empirical work and middle-level theorizing that go into a book like this are often seen by authors as a license for flights

53. *Ibid.*, pp. 282 and 293.

of great theoretical fancy in their concluding remarks. It is as if such books were written so authors would have an excuse to add their commentaries to the accumulated wisdom on the Big Questions posed by the eighteenth- and nineteenth-century founding fathers within the pluralist, elitist and class-hegemony traditions. Such a temptation will be resisted here.

It is sufficient to conclude that this book has attempted to make a case for a class-domination theory of power in America by showing how the ruling class dominates government and the underlying population. It has provided a four-process explanation of the relationship between state and ruling class that can be elaborated, amended or discarded in the light of a variety of empirical examples that journalists and social scientists might wish to examine in the future. It offers a number of direct challenges to pluralist, elitist and Marxian perspectives on the power structure of the United States. In particular, it has shown the pluralist and Marxist paradigms to be wanting on a number of issues. It would thus seem that the onus is upon pluralists and Marxists to develop more adequate explanations of the problems discussed here than they have been able to present in the past.

The weaknesses of certain aspects of the pluralist and Marxist paradigms aside, this book also has shown that the great amount of conflict manifest in American public life is not incompatible with a ruling-class perspective. Conflict within the special-interest process is over narrow issues that do not challenge ruling-class power; in fact, some of these conflicts are between sectors of the business community. Conflict within the policy-formation process, while involving bigger issues, primarily reflects longstanding differences of opinion between moderate and ultraconservative members of the power elite. Only rarely do representatives and allies of the working class raise a significant challenge in this arena, and such challenges either have been beaten back by a united power elite or accommodated by the compromising efforts of the ruling-class moderates. Conflict within the candidate-selection process has been shown to be primarily of a personal nature, seldom involving a critique of class rule. Conflict within the ideology process is often vigorous, but the power elite has been able to keep its opponents from developing their numerous criticisms into an alternative ideology and political program, thus ensuring at least the resigned acquiescence of the majority of the population to the central precepts necessary for the maintenance of ruling-class hegemony.[54]

Although this book shows how the ruling class has been able to dominate government and the underlying population throughout the twentieth century, it recognizes that the struggle for power is a continuous one. Given the contradictions and tensions inherent in capitalism, new problems and challenges constantly arise for leaders within the ruling class, and none of their solutions to these problems and challenges are permanent in nature. Indeed, many of their policies, although successful in the short run or on a specific issue, often breed new tensions because they cannot address fundamental problems. Since the powers that be are not ordained by God, there is always the possibility that an insurgent movement will be able to take advantage of future economic or political conflicts within the system and abolish class rule. Such an eventuality may be as inevitable and imminent as various critics of capitalism have been claiming for the past 130 years, but the working-class political organization that might put an end to class domination in corporate America is not yet in sight.

54. For my suggestions on how the difficult process of challenging ruling-class hegemony might begin, see "Why Socialists Should Be Democrats: A Tactic for the Class Struggle in Corporate America," *Socialist Revolution*, no. 31, January–February, 1977.

INDEX

G. WILLIAM DOMHOFF was born in Youngstown, Ohio, and spent most of his childhood in Rocky River, a suburb of Cleveland. He is the author of *Who Rules America?*, *C. Wright Mills and the Power Elite*, *The Higher Circles*, *Fat Cats and Democrats*, *The Bohemian Grove and Other Retreats*, and *Who Really Rules: New Haven and Community Power Re-Examined*. He is professor of psychology and sociology at the University of California, Santa Cruz.